Perfect Mothe

Susan Van Scoyoc is the clinical director of The Women's Practice in Harley Street, London, and a Chartered Counselling and Health Psychologist. She has been in private practice since 1981 and specializes in counselling women who face problems unique to women and their relationships. In addition to her private practice Susan is active within the Counselling Psychology Division of the British Psychological Society.

Susan is a wife, ex-wife, mother, stepmother, daughter, granddaughter, cousin, niece, aunt, sister, and most of all, herself.

Susan invites readers to visit her web site at
www.invisiblewomen.co.uk

Perfect Mothers, Invisible Women

Susan Van Scoyoc

Robinson
LONDON

Constable & Robinson Ltd
3 The Lanchesters
162 Fulham Palace Road
London W6 9ER

First published in the UK by Robinson,
an imprint of Constable & Robinson Ltd 2000

A copy of the British Library Cataloguing in Publication data for
this title is available from the British Library.

ISBN 1-84119-134-5

Printed and bound in the EU

Contents

Contents

Contents

PART TWO
Making yourself visible: adult mothers

Contents

PART THREE
Fertility, responsibility and work

Contents

PART FOUR
The consequences of change for visible adult mothers

Contents

Acknowledgments

My first words of thanks must, of course, go to my partner Stephen who encouraged, cajoled and even bullied me into writing this book. It started as a magazine article, then he asked "Why not a book?" At first, the task seemed impossible, but Stephen kept on reminding me how much I had to say on motherhood every time I ranted at the television or newspaper. Without his belief in my abilities, I would not have written this book.

Next must be my children, no longer small but very patient and understanding when I disappeared for hours on end. Thank you, Douglas, James and Sarah for showing me how impossible it is to be a perfect mother!

My friends Pam and Dudley have always been ready to discuss ideas, share their hopes and disasters and listen to my own. Between us, we have shared pregnancies and the trials of toddlers, children and adolescence, and through it all, Pam and I have tried not to lose ourselves into invisibility. I think we succeeded.

My thanks also go to my publishers, Constable Robinson Ltd, and especially to Krystyna Green. Her first positive interest in my proposal letter stopped me having an excuse not to continue writing. As she spent the year taking the step from woman to mother, so I took the steps to completing this book.

Acknowledgments

Krystyna and the team at Constable & Robinson have made the publication of this book a pleasure rather than a trial.

Finally, my thanks must go to all the women who told me their stories, trusting me to listen and not criticize. It was these women seeking help through therapy who inspired this book – women trying to cope with the changes and challenges that motherhood brought to their lives, whether new mothers or those facing the moment when their children left home to begin lives on their own. The struggles that these women dealt with had so much in common that this book simply had to be written for all.

Foreword: Family systems thinking

There are some things in life that are universal to us all. Birth and death come to everyone, and all of us experience them within our families. Other events such as marriage, the arrival of children and their leaving home happen to us as we pass through these life stages. The effects of these changes are of particular interest to family therapists.

Family systems theory focuses on relationships between people and on the effects of relatives, other people and the outside world upon the individual.

This awareness of outside influence is what makes family systems theory very different from theories used by other therapists. Rather than focusing on the person who is depressed, the family therapist looks at what is happening within the family, at work and in the rest of the person's world that makes things difficult for him or her. Then the family therapist attempts to change the balances of these influences by encouraging a fresh view of the person within the world. This may mean changing someone's reactions to a pattern of others' behaviour towards them that has lasted for many years. The power of the differing influences changes over time and with circumstances. For example, the influence of the school system on mothers has a great influence during their children's years in education but not before or afterwards.

Foreword

When a woman becomes a mother, she is passing through a life stage. Transforming herself from a single or married woman into a mother is stressful and leads to lots of change. It may result in other people altering their interactions with her. It certainly means the creation of new relationships with medical professionals, school teachers, childcarers, parents and partner.

It is by examining the relationships between the individual and other people – and the influences on them and society as a whole – that it becomes clear how complex being a mother can be.

PART ONE

Perfect mothers:
Caring for others and losing yourself

Motherhood

Perfect mothers

What do we think of when we say we want to be a perfect mother? We think of women playing the idealized role of happy, contented mothers and maybe wives. The image of the perfect mother – standing in the kitchen baking cakes and wiping the baby's nose – comes straight from the 1950s. She breastfeeds and still finds time to look wonderful when her husband returns from the office. She pecks her husband on the cheek and then sits him down to a home-cooked meal. Her children are clean, quiet yet happy.

The perfect mother has no needs of her own, no outside interests that do not contribute to the care of her family. The perfect mother is ready to rush to the aid of any relative in need and still be able to care for her children. She is kind to all and often has her house full of visiting grandparents. The perfect mother is not a sexual being. Her house is always tidy and all is well with the world.

An outdated image, we all say. Of course, this does not happen any more. But what has changed?

Perfect mothers are still those women who spend their lives looking after their children. They stay at home because they choose to put their children first. They sit with their children in the evening, listening to them read and helping with their homework. Their husbands patiently go to work and support the family because that is what is expected of them in this kind of relationship. As a couple, they are often part of a supportive extended family network. Grandparents, uncles and aunts are involved with the family, helping out with babysitting and coming over to visit often. Other women looking at such families think: "If only we could be like them".

Over the years, perfect mothers have been presented to us as the ideal, but is this an image we want to pass on to our own children? The woman who has no needs of her own? The man who is excluded from nurturing relationships within the family and who is secondary to the children? The woman who becomes invisible to her family and the real world once she becomes a mother?

It is time to reconsider the ideal of motherhood. I am suggesting that the perfect mother of the past needs to become just that – a thing of the past. The emotional cost of being a perfect mother on the woman herself and on the family as a whole can be devastating.

The intentions behind women's efforts to be perfect mothers are praiseworthy. Many women want to achieve these ideals. We want to give our children love, attention, support and more. We want to be there for them whenever they need us. We want to be perfect mothers. But we also recognize – or, at least, most of us do – that we cannot be perfect mothers and so we try our hardest instead. We strive and strive and strive, but always fail.

And so we are trapped. Because we cannot be perfect mothers. Because we can always find another woman who appears to be doing a better job at mothering. Because we are bombarded by messages from the media telling us that bad mothers are responsible for all of society's ills. We try harder and yet feel more inadequate.

Carol: the perfect mother but invisible woman?

Carol is the mother of four children. She is the full-time mother with a house full of children. She is the woman who always seems to have family visiting. Everyone loves her children. Everyone helps out. As the moment approaches for her husband Frank, a professional man, to return from work, the household is in chaos with children running all over, loud shrieks and screams echoing through the house. As Frank sits down to his first drink of the evening, Carol is active, almost overactive, as she tries to achieve calm, to put all the children to bed. By the time she comes downstairs to join her husband, she is exhausted. She sits and tells him of her day, which grandparent came to call, and all the latest family gossip.

From a distance, Carol seems to have the perfect family and to be the perfect mother, but to herself, she is a failure. She feels that she does not know how to handle her children. She feels that someone else could do a better job as a mother and a wife. She feels that she rushes all day and still, when her husband returns home, the house is a mess. She feels that all her efforts come to nothing and that she has nothing for herself. Carol feels that she has lost herself. She simply no longer exists within this family. She is the mother of the children. She is the daughter to her own parents and the provider of grandchildren. She is the wife of Frank. Where is there time for Carol? Who *is* Carol?

What happens to a woman when she becomes a mother? What happens if the woman chooses to devote herself to raising her children? What does a woman do when she tries to be the mother that everyone else expects her to be? What does a woman do when she aims to be the ideal perfect mother?

To become that perfect mother, the woman takes on a mantle of invisibility and, in so doing, may become a poor example to her own children.

A new view: becoming an adult mother

In these pages, I will be proposing a new model for women with children to pattern themselves after: the adult mother. The adult mother considers herself and stops doing everything for everyone. The adult mother ensures that she is taken notice of by others and takes care of herself, including making sure that she has time for fun and happiness. The adult mother is the woman who considers her role and relationships with others and makes decisions based on choice rather than un-thinking assumptions.

I also suggest that an adult mother is one who prepares her children to enter the real world. The real world does not con-tain people who are prepared to be personal servants with no needs of their own. A mother who demands nothing for herself and tends to her children's every need sets a poor example for them. The real world contains jobs that demand commitment to regular working hours and sometimes tedious tasks. The real world is not always pleasant. The real world contains other people with whom we have to co-operate and communicate. Our children, whether aged 3 or 13, have to learn how to state their own needs and listen to other people's points of view and share chores and responsibilities – and, of course, have fun being with friends. The role of adult parents is to prepare children to be successful in their entry into the real world.

2

The impossible task: trying to be a perfect mother

Julie: the woman who has everything

Julie came to see me about a year after becoming a mother. She was unhappy but did not know why. She told me she had everything.

"I have a caring husband, a beautiful baby, a lovely house and no money worries. I shouldn't really be here wasting your time, I'm sure there are others who need to see you more than me, but I feel so unhappy. I've felt unhappy for months now and I can't seem to shake it off. My mother says it's just a phase and I expect she is right, but still . . . I just feel I can't go on. I spent all yesterday in tears. I spend a lot of time crying. I don't know why. I just feel empty."

Julie had fulfilled her dream. Her ambition as a young woman had been to be a good wife and mother. She now had a husband who was kind to her and adored their daughter. Why, when she appeared to have everything she ever wanted, was she feeling so awful? I listened to more about her life.

"I'm so miserable. I don't understand it. My mother says I'm jealous of all the attention going to Jessica . . . My husband is such a good father. He works hard. He makes sure we have enough money. He comes home in the evening and takes over looking after our daughter. He loves playing with her. He talks about her all the time and wants to know what she has done during the day."

I asked a little more about Julie's husband. I was interested in how Julie felt about him. She continued to tell me all the good things about him.

"Richard – that's his name – is such a darling. He gets on well with my parents. They think of him as a son. When we go over to their house at the weekend, he talks with my father a lot. My mother tells me how lucky I am to have Richard, what a good father he is to Jessica and what a good husband he is to me. And he is . . . he couldn't be better with Jessica . . ."

Julie sounded as if she was the perfect mother. She stayed at home to look after Jessica and had all the things that many women wish for when having their first child. But read between the lines: everything came back to Jessica or to the opinions of Julie's parents.

I asked Julie about herself. What was she interested in? What did she like to do? The answers were revealing.

"Well, I never really liked my job, so I don't miss that. I only wanted to work until I married and had children. I do miss the company, though. I used to like going out, you know, socializing with my friends, that sort of thing. I really am interested in team sports like basketball. I used to be in some local teams, but I haven't got back into that. I thought I would after Jessica was born, but it's so hard. I'm not fit enough now anyway, I'd never make it back into the old team. I got exhausted just going into town a few months ago."

Julie paused at this point, tears welling up in her eyes. I sat quietly with her for a few moments, watching her composure crumble. The story of her trip into town and its aftermath unfolded through sniffles and, finally, sobs.

Julie took Jessica to her old office one day. Her husband and parents had been concerned that it might be too much for her, struggling into town with the baby, but Julie really wanted to see her old friends and colleagues so she overcame their objections.

Julie thought the day went well. She arrived in the office just before lunch so everyone could see Jessica. It felt really good, showing off her daughter to everyone before she and her closest colleagues went to the local café. It had been a little difficult trying to change Jessica's nappy and feed her there in the crowded café, and Julie had been a bit worried about the smoky atmosphere for Jessica, but all in all, it had been fun.

That evening Julie was exhausted and all she wanted to do was relax, but Jessica was a little cranky – her husband said that it was probably all the excitement and disrupted routine. Jessica did not settle that night, and by the next day, Julie was shattered. So tired, in fact, that she had words with her husband before he left for work that morning. He had not helped the evening before, and had slept through the night while Julie had been up and down trying to stop Jessica from making too much noise and waking him. But, after all, he had an important meeting at work the next day. Before he left for work, Richard asked Julie if she could collect the dry cleaning – he would need his other suit the next day. Julie snapped, asking why he couldn't do it on the way home as he would pass right by the dry cleaner's. Later, of course, she felt guilty and telephoned him at work to say sorry. She would make sure the cleaning was collected, but first she must get some sleep. Perhaps her mother would help.

"It's just a phase you're going through"

As usual, Julie's mother was only too pleased to help as she wanted to spend time with her granddaughter. Julie gratefully went off to bed for an hour. Her mother commented on how the trip into town had disrupted Jessica and how Julie would have to take this into account in the future. Julie was inclined to agree as she wearily climbed the stairs back to bed.

After her rest, she and her mother sat and talked over coffee. Her mother talked about how good Julie was as a mother, how well she was doing to put her daughter and husband first – this was the meaning of motherhood. Her mother seemed genuinely proud of her. Julie felt better, felt she was being recognized for all the effort she was making.

However, despite these words, Julie continued to feel more tired and fed up as the weeks passed. She knew that she loved her daughter and her husband. She kept telling herself that she was lucky. Her mother, her only confidante, told her it was just a phase, it would pass, it was just jealousy, that Julie had always wanted lots of attention and now she was jealous of all the attention Jessica was getting.

"I don't count any more"

Months later, here was Julie, crying into handfuls of tissue before me.

"But I do love her. Jessica means everything to me. I just feel sometimes that no one wants to see me any more. When my mother comes to visit now, it's to see Jessica. I might as well not be there. It's the same when Richard gets home from work. I don't count any more."

Julie had very quickly identified her problem and why she felt so bad inside. She did not feel as though she was important any longer. She had lost herself, as well as her previous relationships with Richard and her mother. Everything had changed. Julie realized that she needed to decide what she wanted.

It took some time to work through the changes that Julie decided she wanted in her life. The start was to recognize that her feelings were not due to something wrong with her as a woman or a mother. Julie was not a bad mother, not jealous or resentful of her daughter. She was not selfish in sometimes wanting to do something for herself. Instead she was reacting to the abrupt change in the way she was treated by those she was now mainly in contact with, especially her husband and parents. The people who were closest to her now saw her as a mother, not as Julie. If Julie did something outside their own view of acceptable behaviour for a mother, such as travelling with Jessica into town, they would point out its negative effects on the little girl, how difficult it would be for her, rather than finding a way to overcome any obstacles.

Julie: finding time for herself

The first thing we discussed was how often Julie actually did something that was just for her, for fun. We talked about what Julie might want for herself in her own future. Julie found this difficult, frequently saying how difficult it would be to find time for herself, how she had to look after Jessica, how she was not sure of what she wanted. Most of all, she questioned whether doing something for herself was selfish and so would make her a bad wife and mother.

To try to break through, I asked the magic question: "Can you see yourself doing the same as you are now – for the next five years?"

Julie looked horrified. "I couldn't stand feeling like this for five years. You're right. I have to do something about this."

From this point, Julie changed. She started to go out one evening and one day a week. She wanted to be an adult mother, and found that leaving Jessica with other people while she went to play basketball did not stop her being a good mother. In fact, she felt that it improved her mood and that she appreciated her time with Jessica more. This was the first and simplest change she could make.

Julie was recognizing herself again as someone with needs of her own. She often asked: "Why did I think I no longer needed anything for me? I wouldn't expect that of anyone else. After Jessica was born, I didn't expect my husband to give up work or going out with his friends once a week. So why did I?"

Always trying to do it right!

I saw Julie as a woman who liked to do things right. To her parents, she was the perfect daughter. Unlike her older sister, whom she described as a disappointment to her parents because of her wayward behaviour and premarital pregnancy, Julie had done things right. She had had the respectable boyfriend with the good career. She had been a virgin bride, living with her parents until the day she married. Julie's parents were very traditional in their views and Julie's husband held the same family values, so initially Julie had felt that this was a perfect match. However, having spent just a few years living this perfect dream marriage, she had arrived at the point in her life when she wanted to make decisions for herself.

Julie recognized that she had accepted all the expectations of her own and her husband's family. These expectations had been Julie's own as she had been raised to see them as *family truths* – for example, the belief that leaving babies with babysitters is bad for children (the actions of bad mothers) or that perfect mothers stay at home and put their children before themselves. However, Julie was now questioning these

12

family assumptions and forming opinions of her own. She stopped believing that family truths were the only way of seeing things. She started to look at all her options concerning her own life and her life as mother and wife, and was ready to make her own judgments.

Talking with parents

Julie decided to confront her parents with how she felt about her relationship with them. She told her mother how much she appreciated her babysitting and the time she was prepared to spend with Jessica, but also spoke of how she herself felt ignored. This was hard for Julie to do, especially as her mother had already told her that, in her opionion, her daughter was jealous of the attention given to Jessica. Julie was prepared for her mother's response, which was to talk about how difficult and demanding Julie had always been.

"I don't feel jealous of Jessica," Julie replied. "I enjoy seeing you with her and know you love her. But I miss the time we used to spend together. I would like to see you sometimes without Jessica. I would sometimes like to have you and Dad over when Jessica is asleep or playing and talk about adult things. I haven't changed even though I'm now Jessica's mother. I'm still Julie, your daughter, and I still need you for me. I also need other things for me. I need to go out alone sometimes. I need time alone with Richard."

Although there was no immediate response from Julie's mother, her daughter's words did have an effect. On their next visit to Julie's former home, both Julie and Richard noticed how both her parents spent more time talking to Julie, asking how she was and what she had done during the week. It was a start.

Working on her marriage

More difficult was Julie's relationship with Richard. As the therapy sessions had gone by, she had begun to talk openly about how empty her relationship with Richard had become. She saw him now as the perfect son-in-law and the perfect father but definitely not the perfect husband or lover. Since Jessica's birth, his only concern seemed to be his daughter. Julie felt invisible even to Richard and, as a result, was beginning to feel angry towards him.

But there was a ray of hope. When, one tearful evening, Julie had first expressed her feelings about her parents ignoring her, Richard had initially been kind but, at the same time, dismissive. He had told her that she was still depressed, that she was perhaps getting things a little out of proportion. However, as the therapy continued and Julie discussed with Richard some of the thoughts and feelings that had arisen during the sessions, he started to notice things for himself – how Julie's parents walked straight past her as they entered the house and went straight to Jessica, and how, when Julie spoke of herself, the subject was always changed to Jessica. Julie had support from Richard regarding her parents. But could she get him to see that she needed the same changes from him?

Julie needed courage and honesty when she spoke with her husband. She used the same basic ideas as she had with her parents. She told Richard that she missed spending time with him and how good it would be to go away together, perhaps for a weekend. Richard's immediate concern was for Jessica. How would she be without both her parents for a weekend? But Julie was persistent. She told Richard that she was sure Jessica would be all right for just 48 hours without them and that, as usual, her parents would love to look after her. Richard was still a little reluctant, but he did agree.

At our next session, Julie was thoughtful about her marriage with Richard. She knew that both she and Richard had wanted a "traditional" marriage. Both had wanted to have children and both had wanted Julie to stay at home and be a perfect mother. Julie and Richard believed that they had a lifestyle that others would envy, and so any unhappiness they felt seemed ungrateful. But Julie now knew that her previous idea of what marriage and motherhood would be like did not match what had actually happened to her. She had some choices to make. For the first time, she was taking responsibility for her own future.

"I realize now that I never made a decision about what I was going to do with myself. I always thought I would get married and so I never thought about a career. I left school at 16 and went straight into secretarial school. When I met Richard, I liked him a lot. He was nice to me and loved me. I wonder now if he loves me more than I love him . . . My parents liked him a lot, too, and it seemed natural to get married. Everyone was so pleased. We married and spent only a few months together before I got pregnant. We never really had time together, just on our own. We hadn't lived together before we married, it wouldn't have been right. Now I wish we had done that. Until now I've just done what was expected of me, whatever seemed to come next."

Taking responsibility for your own future

By making decisions for herself, Julie was taking responsibility for her own future. It is a risky business. It means that Julie will not be able to blame anyone else for what happens to her. She will be responsible for her relationships and her life. Her relationship with Richard will change, too, hopefully for the better. This period of change is preferable to leaving things as they are and allowing resentment and then distance to build up between them. The relationship with her parents will undoubtedly be transformed as Julie begins to state clearly what she wants and how she wishes to be treated.

Julie may decide that she wants to stay at home and raise children, but it will be on her own terms in negotiation with her husband. She will become an individual in her own right rather than just someone's wife, daughter or mother.

Summary of Julie's difficulties and solutions

Julie was facing difficulties shared by many mothers:

- She felt she did not count, so dismissed her own feelings.
- She was expected to put her daughter's needs before her own at all times.
- She no longer knew what she wanted.
- Change seemed impossible.
- Staying the same felt awful.
- Her husband was happy so why wasn't she?
- She recognized that her relationship with Richard was suffering.
- Both her parents and her husband reinforced the ideal of the perfect mother.
- When she tried to change things, the members of her family fought back.

Julie took some definite steps:

- She looked at her own expectations of herself.
- She looked at others' expectations of her.
- She talked with her mother about how she felt.
- She talked with her husband about how she felt.

- She and her husband discussed how to change things for the better.

Part Two offers help and detailed guides on how to take some of these steps yourself.

3

The influence of family on our style of motherhood

We learn a huge amount of what we know from our family. Think about all those early years of training to enter the world. For most of us, that preparation for our adult life is carried out within our family. The family can consist of one main parent, the traditional two parents and brothers and sisters, a blended family of step-parents, step-brothers and step-sisters or an extended family of aunts, uncles and grandparents. In our early years, we are taught things that we then carry with us into adulthood. These family truths and family rules can remain unquestioned within us because we have neither recognized their influence nor challenged their validity.

When we reach the age of five or so, we start at a local school. Outside influences enter our lives. We see children from different types of families. We meet teachers who may open – or close – our minds. Each day we leave our families and go out to encounter the outside world. Each evening we return home to the same families and their constant influence.

We see our own families as normal. It doesn't matter what our families are like or what the members collectively believe. In our own families, we find all the things we are used to. Our own styles of behaviour as mothers, the way we praise or discipline our children, are learned from our own families. We look at other families and see them as too strict or too relaxed. Our parents make comments, without a second thought, about other families, such as those of our school friends: "Sharon's mother isn't like us, dear. She dates all those men from the soccer club ..." In our early years at school, our parents encourage us to mix with other children who are similar to ourselves. When the mothers meet for coffee, acceptance of each other occurs when they find that their families are similar in structure and style.

Where does this leave us when we reach adulthood? It leaves us accepting as inevitable or normal things that we should probably question. As adults, we may think that we have formed our own opinions, but until we look at our family truths with opened eyes, we are still reacting as if we are children. We are not making our own independent decisions and so not acting as adult mothers. And women are particularly vulnerable to the influence of family truths because of the life-long expectation placed on them that they will conform more and be more considerate to others.

When we make decisions: why family influence is important to recognize

As we leave home and go out into the world, we may assume that we are leaving our families and all their rules behind. We spend time with our friends, take lovers, find homes of our own and live our own lives. We think we have become adults.

Later we find a career, maybe settle down with a partner, even get married and have children of our own. We think that we have developed adult, independent lives of our own.

Then comes the day when we suddenly realize that something we have said sounds just like something our mothers have said, or that a particular phrase we have used is the very one we hated to hear spoken by our parents when we were teenagers. Or we realize that we are deciding to do things that we really don't want to do. This is often felt at Christmas when, instead of going off on holiday with friends, or staying at home with our children and relaxing by the fire, we face the seemingly endless rounds of visiting parents and parents-in-law. Even if we have announced in November that we will not be coming to the traditional family get-together, the pressure to join in, to not disappoint others, stops us doing what we might want to do. What is happening here?

Your exclusive club membership

Without ever knowing it, you have become a member of an exclusive club! This is your family club, which has rules for and expectations of its members. Some members have a lot of influence over how the others behave, and some have almost no influence at all. Some members group together and form alliances, while others constantly battle over the slightest thing. The members of this exclusive club all know the rules; they all know who to be careful not to offend and who will always be there to lend a shoulder to cry on. For all the members of this club, some behaviours or choices are simply unthinkable.

The club operates a little like a religious sect. Members might leave and refuse to come back to celebrate family rituals such as Christmas with the rest of the family club, but the lapsed members retain their family club beliefs, which causes guilt and influences their decisions for the rest of their lives.

For those members who follow the club rules, life can be comfortable, safe and predictable. It will remain this way as long as no rules are broken or the hierarchy challenged.

The family club tries to keep everything the same. It is more comfortable for everyone this way. Generation after generation may have been members of this exclusive club, and the expectations of everyone remain steady. If the club is very child oriented, the most successful and popular members of the club will be those with young children; grandparents will be proud of their grandchildren and may even begin to value them more than their own adult children. If the club is very career orientated, the most successful and popular members of the club will be the lawyers and doctors, even if they are rude and opinionated.

Most family clubs have a mix of rules. What might be acceptable for some members might be completely unacceptable for others. Boisterousness from the young male members might be seen as high spirits, while the same behaviour in a group of married mothers might be seen as disgraceful!

How do family clubs operate?

Automatic membership of the family club comes by being born into it. The old saying "You can choose your friends but you can't choose your family" sums it up. You are a member of this exclusive club whether you like it or not.

The older members of the club are usually the ones with the greatest influence. This is usually the mother and father but it can be the grandparents before they become old and infirm or a powerful aunt or uncle.

Honorary membership of the family club comes if you marry in, or perhaps if you live with one of the members, or if you share the parenting of a child with an existing member. This honorary membership can be as binding as automatic membership, or it might be temporary.

Honorary members are often chosen, quite unconsciously, by existing members because they possess all the qualities to make them acceptable to the family club. Thus a son may choose a wife who is strong minded like his mother. Although this may appear to bring conflict to the club, in that the mother and daughter-in-law constantly clash and argue, it actually provides the son with the type of woman he knows how to handle and the father knows how to placate the daughter-in-law. So all the behavioural interactions of the members settle down into disharmonious harmony.

All the interactions of the members of the club need to be seen in terms of their effect on everyone belonging to it. A difficult, bossy mother might serve to keep the younger members in line and so relieve the quieter father of that responsibility. Even though the father may complain that he has had no hand in dealing with the children, he does not step forward to involve himself. Instead he chooses to settle into his role and allow his wife to continue her reign. The children respond by becoming more afraid of the mother and learning that they can safely confide in their father. The family club maintains its balance as the mother and father complement each other. Between them, they run their club by offering vital things that the younger members need to grow: rules and someone to confide in.

Thinking about your own family club

Before you can be a true independent adult, it is important that you examine your own membership in your family club. Consider the following questions, which will help you to tease out the way in which your club operates.

- Who is seen as the one to go to for advice?
- Whose disapproval is the most difficult to handle?
- From whom will many members keep secrets (for whatever reason)?

- Who is seen as the most successful member of your club? Why?
- Who is seen as the biggest failure of your club? Why?

The membership of your family club costs nothing in monetary terms but may extract a huge hidden cost if its influence is not recognized.

Why are families so impossible?

Family relationships are often troublesome, and conflicts between the same members of the family can recur year after year. This may not make any sense, even to the individuals involved, but if you look at the family as a whole, as a club with its own rules, you may be enlightened.

The main aim of a family club is to maintain the status quo. If you look at any group of people operating together, you will discover that the members find it more comfortable to stay the same and only deal with what is familiar. In families, where everyone knows each other well, the individual members interact with each other in ways that are familiar to them – even if these interactions are upsetting. We all have relatives who can "press our buttons" to evoke an outburst within seconds. The import of the simple words exchanged between you may not be understood by an outsider, someone who is not a member of the club, who looks on in wonder at the extreme reaction they produce.

The family club members are reacting like this – with those exchanges of words, or even fists – because this behaviour is familiar to them. The father who fights with his adolescent son is attempting to keep the control he had when the boy was younger, to keep the interaction between himself and his son on familiar ground. He may even be repeating the same interactions he had as an adolescent with his own father. The mother who acts as mediator between the father and son, attempting to maintain the peace between them, is actually preventing change, whether for better or worse.

Families are closed clubs that follow patterns. Generation after generation, the members obey the same club rules and pass on the same expectations of its members. If your grandmother and mother worked while raising their families, the chances are that you will do the same. It is as if this is the role expected of you. If your grandmother and mother stayed at home to raise their children, this, too, may be the role expected of you, even if you and they do not realize it.

The effects of major events within the family can be far reaching and hidden. The woman who lost her own mother to cancer at the age of 35 may feel a hidden pressure to achieve everything before this age. As she approaches it, she may find herself unable to cope and cling to her own children. She has no concept of life after 35. In fact, she is accepting what she believes unconsciously is her fate as a woman member of this family – and she is giving the same message to her own children. Her daughter may find herself struggling as she, too, approaches 35. Her son may have difficulties in his relationship with his partner as she nears that significant age.

By recognizing the importance of understanding our family clubs, we can expose hidden and unspoken family truths, which can permeate through the lives of all the members.

Family truths and women

Eileen was preparing a rump roast one day. Her eight-year-old daughter watched as she took her sharpest knife and cut a slice about half an inch thick from the one end of the piece of beef. "Why do you do that?" asked the little girl. Eileen thought for a moment and answered, "I don't know . . . I suppose because your grandmother always did it and she taught me how to cook."

The next time Eileen's parents visited, her mother watched Eileen cooking in the kitchen, just as Eileen had watched her mother for many years and as her daughter had only a few weeks before. Eileen remembered her daughter's question about preparing the roast and asked her mother, "Why do you cut the slice off the end of the roast? I've done it for years without knowing why."

"You have?" said her mother. "But, dear, I only did that because the roast wouldn't fit into our old roasting tin!"

This amusing story highlights how powerful family truths can be in our lives. Eileen had always behaved in a certain way without being aware of the origin of at least one of the truths in her own family club.

The family as a whole needs to be understood, rather than the behaviour of an individual member at a particular time. The family is the most powerful and influential club we are ever likely to belong to. The ways in which its members function physically, socially and emotionally are profoundly interdependent. If change takes place in any one member or section of the family club, the effects ripple out to impact on other members or sections. Nothing happens in isolation. Where you fit into this family club influences your life choices, who you believe you are and the relationships you form when establishing your own family.

So where do women fit within these family clubs? The hidden message that is learned by women in the families that seem to be admired most – traditional extended families – is to maintain these families. The men are encouraged to grow and to find careers for themselves, which allows them to become more individualized adults, or to awaken, earlier than women. However, the women, who on the surface may be encouraged to have careers, have also been raised with the idea of maintaining the family.

Thus it is the woman in a couple who usually buys the birthday cards and Christmas gifts for members of both her partner's and her own family. It is the woman who cares for others, such as the elderly or seriously ill. It is the woman who is encouraged to help keep things on an even keel. The effect on the other members of the family is simple – her actions mean that life can carry on as normal. Other members can continue to go to school, go to work or carry out other aspects of their lives. The woman who provides the care ceases going to work or college and helps maintain the status quo for all the others. Or she tries to balance it all, going to work and adding to her daily itinerary the care of, say, an ill parent or relative.

Ironically, women like this are also often the harshest critics of those who attempt to escape from family traditions. These women maintain the moral vanguard for the family and act as advisers to the next generation – family truths are constantly restated to remind younger female family members how to be good women as well as perfect mothers. These women are the first to heap criticism on anyone who does not play their role in the family or steps out of line. They voice the hurt and betrayal felt by the rest of the family. They are the family's mouthpiece.

There is a *golden rule* to remember when thinking about yourself and your own membership of the family club: those who try to change are subject to pressure from the family to stop changing and return to their old selves.

Absolute truths from the family and beyond

The absolute truths within a family are presented as fact, and so have even more power than family beliefs. They represent the true values of the family club. Absolute truths are so ingrained in families that their influence is unseen and unquestioned. We fail to recognize that we have blindly accepted as absolute truths the general pattern of life handed down to us by our families and those social values that the family club adopts. Therefore, we follow patterns of behaviour and make choices that are acceptable to the family club. We do not question what is actually the family club's value system, not our own, seeing anything that challenges these absolute truths as wrong. It is only when absolute truths are examined one by one that you can decide for yourself whether you accept or reject them.

Here are some absolute truths commonly found in family clubs:

- A normal woman will want children of her own.
- A woman cannot expect to keep a man if she refuses him a child.
- The woman who is infertile has failed in her duty to reproduce.
- The fertile woman who chooses not to have a child is selfish.
- A woman's most fulfilling moment is when her newborn baby looks into her eyes.
- A woman does not really feel love until she has a baby of her own.
- A woman shows her most unselfish love when raising a child.
- A woman always puts her children first.
- Men cannot look after children as well as women.
- (Grand)Mother always knows best.
- A woman stays at home with her young children.
- A woman is at home when her children return from school.
- A woman goes to all school plays, assemblies, parents' evenings.

- A woman does not allow her job to interfere with being a mother.
- A woman does not leave her children to go out and have fun herself.

Women and men are raised surrounded by these family club values, which subsequently influence their views of themselves. But it is the women who bear the burden of many of these absolute truths. It is the women, rather than their male partners, who are asked by friends and family whether they will have children. It is the women who are assumed to have a strong desire to have children. It is the women who are pressured to be ideal perfect mothers. It is only when these same women are overwhelmed by the impossibility of trying to live by these truths that they say, "Enough! I can't do all this!" It is at this moment that women begin to look at what it means to be an adult mother. It is now that women look at ways of making their own decisions and taking responsibility for themselves.

4

What am I doing? I can't do all this!

At some point in our lives as mothers, we look around us and wonder what we're doing. We wonder how we've ended up with the lives we have. We are trying to be the best mothers we can, perfect mothers as well as possibly balancing both a career and a relationship with a partner. It is as if we've been struggling to do the impossible for too long. We wake up with a jolt and realize it can't be done, that trying to balance everything for much longer is impossible – everything is going to come tumbling down. We run around trying to get it right. We believe that there is a right way and a wrong way to be a mother. There are perfect mothers and bad mothers. There are good wives and bad wives. There are good women and bad women. We do not acknowledge the fact that all these individuals are struggling to be women and mothers and doing the best they can.

Some women at this time are so afraid of what they see in their own lives and what they feel within themselves that they avoid looking ever again. Those who are frightened like this settle down into the role given to them: that of perfect mothers but invisible women.

Working mothers often believe that they are failing as perfect mothers. Even if these women feel that they are bad mothers, they strive to be regarded as perfect mothers, putting their own needs after work and home life. Rather than face up to changes that might make things easier, they choose to leave things alone, never awakening to their own needs or their own potential.

If we are to awaken to our true selves and to the responsibilities we have to ourselves, we need courage – and lots of it. Because if we take a hard look, with our eyes wide open, we may not like some of the things that we once saw as giving us stability. We may look and see that the soft, seducing bedrock of our life also prevents us from doing things that will give us other pleasures, other means of fulfilment. It may be that our security in knowing what will make us good women and perfect mothers to our children is also destroying us inside. It may be making us invisible to ourselves and to the outside world.

You may find that your relationships with others, including your partner, parents or work colleagues, begin to improve following this realization. You may come to recognize that you need to make changes in the way you communicate your own needs and wants, as well as listen to others more. Most importantly, you need to be seen and heard, by others and yourself. Women who have lost themselves often suffer most in families and in society because of their invisible status.

Waiting for your turn

For most of their lives and for generation after generation, women have put others before themselves. I see women in therapy who have awakened to this fact in their 20s, others when they reach their 70s. In each and every case is the dawning realization that they waited for their turn but it had never come. They now see that it is only going to be their turn if they take it. No one will ever give you your turn, especially if they don't know you are waiting for it. No one will give you your turn while you remain invisible.

We all know women who are caring for others. We applaud this in our society and call these women good. They care for their children, or their parents, or their grandchildren, and derive pleasure and reward from doing so. However, behind this image is a hidden cost. Perhaps the real problem is that women do not voice their own wants and needs. They think that these are unimportant, only to be considered after everyone else's wants and needs have been met. The question "What do you want?" is one they are not used to being asked; still less do they think about it.

Women are raised with a weakness: they do not say clearly what they want because they do not expect to get it. As a result, their needs are not considered as having equal merit compared to others in the family or in society. Many women choose to care for others. However, if they do make this choice, it should be made freely, not forced, then endured or resented. Women may blame everyone else for their unhappiness and their position. Is this fair? Should women take responsibility for their own needs and ensure they as individuals are seen and heard?

Women who are seen but not heard: becoming invisible

Are women invisible in our society? Why are their needs and opinions rarely sought? Women as a sex are considered and recognized more now than at any other time. However, the majority of individual women are still unseen and unheard. We may have worked towards equal rights in the world of employment, social clubs and so on, but speak with a group of 20 women who work and have male partners: the majority will reveal that they have to rush home from work to prepare the evening meal, help the children with their homework and do the ironing. Have we actually improved the lot of women or, by expecting women to be equal in the workplace without compensatory moves in their personal lives, have we condemned women to a living hell?

It is in their individual lives that women face fundamental problems because of their upbringing. Women are raised to be reserved and to be guided by others. One of the consequences of an awakening is making your own decisions. This is something women are less experienced at doing than men. It is no one's fault. Society has developed around the idea of the man being responsible and making family decisions, with the woman remaining at home as carer, usually of the children of the couple, while being supported financially by the man. The source of this scenario may be obscure or obvious, but it is not the role of this book to explore the history of our society. However, the taking on of such responsibility by men has taken its toll on both men and women.

So many of the women I see in therapy have not made their own decisions or taken responsibility for their lives. They have consulted with others until they have a consensus of opinion. They ask their friends, their parents, their children and their partners what they should do next. They fret when they hear differing pieces of advice. They worry and worry until they find advice that is backed by the most people, which they then act on. Women rarely consider what they want for themselves alone. All they know is that, for years, they have been unhappy, or tired, or resentful.

It is hard to change and begin to consider one's own wants and needs. Women who awaken to their own needs face taking on the responsibility of making themselves happier.

What am I doing? I can't do all this!

The story of Rose, awakened at 70

Rose is a 70-year-old living at home with her mother, for whom she has cared for most of her life. Long ago, there had been what Rose saw as her one chance to leave home, back when she was in her early 30s. However, no one else would put up with her mother's outbursts of temper, and the man who had asked her to marry him had not been prepared to have her mother live with them. So Rose had decided to stay where she was.

Now, having reached 70, Rose felt that she could no longer cope. Decades of anger and resentment at never being asked what she wanted by her large number of brothers and sisters all came spilling out. As I sat with her, I was not surprised by the anger, the resentment or the sadness of wasted opportunity. However, I was surprised by her determination to change. Perhaps it was because she had suddenly become aware of the short time left to her, though her own mother was in her 90s, that she became determined to make the most of everything. She made hard decisions and took responsibility for them.

Rose decided to continue caring for her mother. She recognized that her whole life had been given over to this task and to walk away from it now would be too hard for her and devastating for her mother. However, she now drew some limits. She made it clear that, if her mother became any more infirm, she would have to be cared for by someone else. She also gave herself set "days off", when others would have to sit with her mother while she went out. And go out she did. Rose started with visits around the town in which she lived, then travelled further afield by train. Her reservations about doing things she had never done before soon gave way to the excitement of the theatre and bright lights.

The consequences of her decisions were dealt with one by one. Rose coped with her mother's tears and with angry phone calls from relatives accusing her of selfishness. She was as clear with her relatives as she had been with me when she said that she had decided to change her life.

Who owns the problem?

It is easy to assume responsibility for things that are not ours. Rose took on the responsibility for her mother's unhappiness and dependence. In doing so, she shouldered the problem herself and her brothers and sisters did not have to share it with her. Rose became an honorary perfect mother!

Within the family club, and especially in the role of perfect mother, many women take on problems that should actually be shouldered by someone else. Later you will read about Anne (*see* page 67), who dealt with someone else's problem – her husband's relationship with his mother. Thomas had transformed his own reluctance to deal with his mother into pressure on Anne to socialize with her. This assuming of other people's problems is a common phenomenon, especially in women's lives. We try to prevent other people from becoming upset. We try to maintain relationships between others in the family. We act as mediators without realizing that our mediation prevents the two people involved sorting out their own differences and coming to an agreement.

It is an important step when you are able to look at your difficulties and see which problems are yours to work on and which have nothing to do with you. A problem that is not yours should be handed back to the person who owns it. "Who owns the problem?" is a question that should be asked whenever difficulties seem insoluble. When other people are the reason why you can't do what you want to do, or when others are the reason why you can't change something that needs changing in your life, you need to ask: "Who really owns the problem?"

It helps to have an understanding of how families work so that the pressures and relationships can be understood. To help yourself look at your own family, reread Chapter 3.

Change is difficult

If you are unhappy, there may be many reasons why. However, finding the source of your unhappiness might be more than you can manage alone. If, after all your own efforts, you still feel as confused as you did when you started, consult a therapist. It need not take years in therapy to resolve certain difficulties. It may only take a few visits, sharing your thoughts with someone who is not involved in any way in your life. A few thoughtful questions or comments may make everything clear.

Once you have spent time identifying what is causing your unhappiness, you can choose to do something about it or not. Change is difficult. There is no way to make it easier. However, what many people do not realize is that it may be equally difficult to remain the same.

Change is also difficult for others. Other people may find your changes threatening or at least not understandable. They may try to keep their relationship with you the same as it has always been. Staying the same is easier for them than changing with you. The main thrust of a group or club, whether family members or colleagues at work, is to keep things the same. This gives a whole new meaning to the idea that you only need to look at a woman's mother to see what the woman will become later in life!

You should recognize that anything you do that is new to your family or to your partner is inherently threatening. So if

35

your mother did not work and you decide that you are going to pursue a career, you may find yourself on the receiving end of lots of supposedly helpful "advice". These negative comments are relatively easy to deal with when they are out in the open and so easily countered. It is the hidden messages that are harder to deal with. A clue that you are receiving such messages is when you feel low and drained after a conversation.

Look again at what happened to Julie in Chapter 2. When Julie's mother came to help out the day Julie was so exhausted after her trip into town, it seemed as if she was receiving from her mother both practical help and praise for being a perfect mother. But look more carefully at what was said.

After her rest, Julie and her mother sat and talked over coffee. Her mother talked about how good Julie was as a mother, how well she was doing to put her daughter and husband first – that was the true meaning of motherhood, she said. Her mother seemed genuinely proud of her. Julie felt better, believing that all the efforts she had been making were being recognized.

However, Julie's husband and parents seem to be part of all the decisions Julie made. She had travelled into town despite all their concerns, which had been focused on her daughter Jessica, but read between the lines and see how Julie had been told that going into town with Jessica would be the action of a bad mother. On her return, the family club had taught her the consequences of making the decision against their good advice. Her husband had been unsupportive that night so that Julie would have to bear the full consequences of being a bad mother. His support and co-operation would have made a world of difference to Julie and to their relationship.

Julie's mother had offered apparent support but used it to give advice on being a perfect mother. The message had been clear: to be a perfect mother means putting husband and child first – always. To avoid ending up in the exhausted mess that she had been the next day, Julie should have put her daughter first.

Notice that Julie had felt that she was being praised. But, in fact, there was a deeply negative hidden message: stop doing things for yourself. It was the conflict between this hidden message and Julie's attempts at changing her social life that caused her to feel more and more depressed. The changes she had started to put into effect with her own parents and husband would lead to her becoming recognized as a separate person. She was beginning to make decisions for herself. Yet some of these decisions would conflict with those made by other members of her family club or even her wider social group.

Taking responsibility for choices: becoming an adult

Women try to please others and not offend. By not voicing an opinion about what you want, you are making a choice – a choice of omission, a choice to remain silent. We often expect our partners, our parents or our children to know what we want – or we decide their needs are more important than ours. As a result, we become quiet and withdrawn, depressed and resentful without taking responsibility for saying what we need. We have regarded our own needs as secondary for so long that we believe ourselves to be without need. We have become invisible, even to ourselves. It is with our awakening that we women grow to responsibility and adulthood.

As adults, we should be ready to take responsibility for our own choices – even when the consequences are unpleasant. However, we usually encounter mixed consequences. We may choose to do or say something that is positive for us, only to find that other people are offended. Or we may choose to say something to please someone else and then find ourselves repeatedly doing something that we don't like because no one else knows how much we hate and resent it.

Rose tried to please her family and ease her sense of family responsibility when, as a younger woman, she took on the care of her mother. She did have a choice. She could have told her family that she was going to marry and that someone else would have to be responsible for their mother. She did not. Rose did not voice her resentment or frustration, so other members of the family assumed that she was content caring for their mother and they offered to help less and less. Rose put others first. But she also chose to care for her mother because she feared that her guilt at leaving would perhaps be greater than the pain of losing her fiancé. Whatever happened in the beginning, the consequences for Rose were profound until she was prepared to say, "Enough!" and to act as the adult woman she was. It was only when Rose reached her 70s that she truly grew up and took responsibility for herself. Until then it was always someone else's responsibility and someone else's fault.

When women awaken, they become adults. Awakening is a time of looking around as an individual responsible for your own life. Your parents are no longer making choices for you – or they should not be. Your partner or friends should not be deciding how your life will turn out. No religion or organization should dictate choices to you. The only person in control of your life should be you. You may choose to please your family. You may choose to please a partner or friends. You may choose to abide by religious or organizational rules. But the choice is yours, no one else's.

Women tend to make this transition to full adulthood at a later stage than men. Why? Because they are protected. In expecting women to be caring and responsible for others, society also absolves women of responsibility for themselves. The older generation takes care of women, making sure they are safe and secure. Male partners protect and care for their women, taking on these responsibilities without realizing that this removes choice from these apparently adult females. Even today, some "caring" husbands undermine their wives' attempts to go out to work because they believe that they should remain at home and care for the children. Women are placed in a helpless, dependent position while at the same time being expected to care for children and the elderly. They bear responsibility without being seen as responsible for themselves. If they make a decision to act outside of the pattern of behaviour expected of them, they are seen as irrational or crazy and therefore not responsible for their actions.

Adult mothers rather than perfect mothers

What does this mean to women who are mothers? For those who have awakened to their own lives, there is also a fresh look at motherhood. If a woman is no longer content to be invisible, she must question her striving to be a perfect mother.

What are we trying to do for our children? It seems to me that, after we care for them while they are completely helpless, we start to teach them how to survive. We teach them not to push their fingers into light sockets. We teach them how to cross the road. We teach them how to survive until their next birthday . . . and the next . . . and the next. At the same time we attempt to teach social skills. How to behave in company soon becomes very important for toddlers. As they grow into teenagers, the things they need to learn and the things they need from their mothers change.

The fundamental task of parents is to prepare children for real life in the outside world. This can only be done by adult mothers who do not attempt to wait on their children like servants and protect them from all ills like guardian angels. Adult mothers teach their children how to look after themselves and how to cope with living with others. Sharing and co-operation become part of the adult mother's household.

5

The path to motherhood

If we become mothers, we all want to be *perfect* mothers. It would be unthinkable for any woman who has just given birth to tell herself or others that she intends to be a bad mother. So all women who choose to have children have a common goal: to be perfect mothers. What one woman means by "perfect mother" may be completely different from what another woman means. But perhaps the ideal is not very different, even in women from very different backgrounds.

For most women, the ideal mother is one who stays at home with her children when they are very young and, later, is there when they return from school, who cooks and cleans, helps her children with their homework and is generally available to them 24 hours a day.

Where does this ideal come from? How are women moulded into this universal self-sacrificing ideal? What is it that drives women who become mothers to disappear from view? Why do these women become invisible – even to themselves?

The early years: creating little mothers

The birth of a daughter

When infants are born, they become new members of the family club. When girls are born, they are loved, they are wanted, but within the family club, they often have no value in their own right. A girl is seen for what she will bring in terms of caring for others and her later ability to be a perfect mother, so adding new members to the family club. But caring and motherhood often come low on a list of a family club's priorities. Think of the difference between the announcement, even today, that a newborn baby is a boy rather than a girl: "It's a boy!"

Jill was on the telephone to her parents to tell them of the birth of her son.

"Well done, dear. How wonderful and you did it the right way round."

"What do you mean, the right way round?"

"You had your son first. Your sister had Annie first and then Timmy. I know it doesn't matter these days, but it is nice to have a son first, don't you think?"

With these words, the family's hierarchy and its expectations of gender roles are laid out for all to see. It is at the time of a birth that families come together and often, unwittingly, reveal family truths. For example, the importance of the family name is discussed at the birth of the first boy of the next generation. Family lines are said to "die out" when there is no male born to "carry on the name". The family views itself as dead if there are only females born in a generation.

In rich or powerful families, the pressure to produce a male heir is obvious and often openly spoken about. For instance, the combined joy and relief of Indira Gandhi's mother at having just successfully given birth to a healthy child was shattered when she heard her own mother moan: "It should have been a boy!"[1] To some extent we may accept or even understand this. It merely demonstrates a socially acceptable invisibility of women in families.

We could reassure ourselves by remembering that the reaction of Indira Gandhi's grandmother occurred several generations in the past and in India. Surely such a dismissal of the birth of a girl would only occur abroad? After all, the Chinese custom of binding girls' feet, the infanticide of newborn girls by exposing them to the elements or even the elective termination of female foetuses are things that only happen thousands of miles away. We reassure ourselves that our society no longer holds such deep-seated prejudices.

However, we should not feel so comfortable. We simply have to look at the birth of Princess Diana. Her parents had expected and wanted a boy. It took them a week to decide on a name for her as they had not considered girls' names before her birth. Diana herself said, "I was supposed to be a boy." Following the birth of three daughters, Diana's mother was sent to a clinic to establish why she was not conceiving and delivering a son.[2]

We could still regard this as something that happens in families who are hopelessly stuck in the past. One would have thought that this bias against having daughters had disappeared by now. After all, Diana was born nearly 40 years ago. But once again we would be mistaken.

Within the last decade, studies have confirmed that 70–90% of parents still prefer a boy as the firstborn.[3] Interestingly it is the mothers who display a slightly stronger preference for firstborn sons than their male partners. Is this because the woman knows the disadvantages of being a woman or is it that family expectations have become more entrenched in these women?

Read these words, written to an agony aunt in January 1999 by a man asking advice on whether things will be better in a second marriage, even though he had not finished with the first: "We have one daughter who I am not interested in. I wanted a son but she couldn't even do this for me. I have told her she is a bad wife."[4]

The evidence for an anti-female bias shouts at us from our own television screens. During the lead-up to Christmas 1998, a leading toy manufacturer advertised on television in the UK. The theme of the advertisements was brief but very much to the point. The scene opens with a man holding a newborn baby in his arms and making racing-car noises to what we now assume is a boy. Suddenly a nurse comes over and reprimands the father, asking him what he is doing with this baby. Meanwhile we see a forlorn, neglected-looking woman holding a baby daughter, or so we assume as the baby is dressed in pink. The nurse's voice tells the father to go back to his wife and daughter. The caption to the campaign (and there were other advertisements in the same vein) was: "Scalextric™ – it's a male thing." The message is clear: daughters are boring while sons are fun.

How much does this apply to our own families? How often have we heard, or do we remember hearing, these age-old comments when a new baby has been born? Are similar things spoken aloud by members of our family club? How often are different members of the family compared? What does it mean when we hear "she looks just like Granny Jones" or "he is the spitting image of Uncle George"? Can we choose the way we raise our sons and daughters or are we stuck within ever-repeating family patterns? Can we choose what kind of mother we want to be?

I think that we *can* make a choice, but to do so, we need to be aware of the strong influence that the family club and family truths have on our own behaviour. Once we know how to deal with that, we can then choose how we want to be as women and mothers. Who said being a parent would be easy?

We cannot change all of society overnight. The feminist movement has been unable to alter the fundamentals of society in more than three generations, although it has highlighted difficulties and led the way. The greatest direct influence on society comes from the family, from within the family. A colleague of mine, a self-declared feminist, will tell virtually anyone about her views, and will point out when others' behaviour or speech betrays an unawareness of women's issues. But when she is faced with her own family at Christmas, she – by her own admission – bites her tongue and steps back into her shell, becoming passive and compliant. She becomes invisible and behaves like a good wife and daughter. Her family knows that she is not like the rest of them, but within their circle, she is expected to behave and keep all of "those" opinions for her university friends. She behaves as the family club rules dictate.

It is within our own families and within ourselves that the change must begin. It is here that change is at its most effective but is also the hardest to instigate. My colleague may be a feminist at work and in her private life, but faced with the expectations of her family at Christmas, she feels powerless to resist. At the same time, she is unhappy with herself because she knows that this is her weakness, the one time she feels completely unable to say "no". Some day she may find the courage to say it and take responsibility for her own choices and her own pleasure at Christmas. But until then she is allowing herself to be trapped by the family club.

Gender training from the cradle

From the beginning of life, girls and boys are treated differently, and the differences we expect to see in the "different sexes" are emphasized and reinforced. Families celebrate, or not, the entry of a new member to their exclusive club. The birth of a daughter is marked with pink cards and comments on how adorable she looks, while the arrival of a son is marked with blue cards and remarks that he has a strong grip or a gusty wail. From the outset, the daughter is described in terms of how she appears, how she may interact with others, her passive qualities. The boys are complimented on their active qualities, such as how much noise they can make or how strong they can grip. The boys are given control, the power to influence their environment, but the girls are not given this option.

Once you are aware of this difference – the active male and the passive female – the message hits you time after time. Of course, there are now newspaper and magazine articles, television programmes and books that attempt to redress the balance, but the overwhelming message is that it is right to preserve what we are comfortable with: the status quo.

What does this tell us? Certainly it communicates that it is more fun to be a boy – the active, adventurous life is definitely more thrilling. That boys are preferable to girls? That only boys can play with such exciting toys? That girls are naturally more nurturing and it is their destiny to become perfect mothers? Does the message extend as far as implying that having a daughter is a failure on the mother's part, so that she will be forlorn and neglected? The Scalextric™ advertisement unashamedly declared all these things. However, the message is usually conveyed more subtly and is therefore more insidious.

From the moment they are born, girls are trained to be invisible, to be seen and not heard. They are encouraged to look good and behave well, and behaving well usually means being accepting of others. They are taught from the cradle to become perfect mothers – passive, giving and gracious.

Boys are dressed most carefully even as newborns and in their early years. This seems to run counter to the accepted idea that it is the outward appearance of girls that is of the greatest importance, until you realize that the boys' parents do not want their sons to be mistaken for girls. To mistake a boy for a girl is far more embarrassing than to mistake a girl for a boy. It has even been suggested that this over-reaction in boys' parents is due to a fear of homosexuality or confused gender identity in their sons (who are than only a few weeks or months old!). By contrast, infant girls are dressed in clothes that are often "unisex" in nature. Perhaps it is an advantage for a baby girl to be mistaken for a boy and so take part in those active games!

How are women trained to be invisible? It begins early, with the first gifts of toys and clothes. The toys given to little girls invite nurturing – babies requiring dressing, feeding and changing – or carrying out household duties: shopping trolleys, vacuum cleaners or kitchen sets. All these are toys designed to turn them into perfect mothers. The boys have action toys – they drive their toy cars, play with swords or build with Lego™.[5] The boys play only for their own pleasure and take risks with their toys, focusing away from family and home.

Even in the first year of life, the treatment and expectations of boys and girls are different. As crawling and toddling begins, the distance that girls are allowed to wander is more limited than boys of the same age. Girls are expected to stay close to home and family and curb their exploring, adventurous instincts. Even the clothing in which we dress infants encourages the differences. Frilly dresses serve their purpose to restrict and make passive, and emphasize daughters' appearance.

After the first few months of life, parents handle their sons more roughly in preparation for the knocks and tumbles of exploration and risk. Boys are encouraged to explore, to be adventurous and to escape from their mothers' skirts to the world beyond.[6] Their (obviously male) clothes are rugged and practical to encourage movement and getting dirty. They are expected to develop the independence that much later will enable them to leave home to fend for themselves – unlike their sisters.

The infant girl is raised with the expectation of dependence as well as of nurturing. Most people still hope to raise a daughter until it is time for her to find a man and be married into dependency on him. Fathers often have a feeling of extra responsibility towards their female offspring, becoming "fairy godfathers" to their daughters.

As they grow, girls are given chores that are likely to be focused on the home, such as washing dishes or vacuuming, while their brothers are more likely to be asked to shovel snow or help repair the car. This separation of masculine and feminine tasks serves to maintain the status quo into the next generation. Boys become skilled at outdoor, technical, "masculine" chores, whereas girls learn that they are not as good at them as their brothers (through lack of experience or teaching). However, boys regard washing dishes or vacuuming as easy jobs and thus continue to devalue the only chores their sisters and, later, their partners are expected to do.

What does this mean to girls as they grow up to be women? They learn to expect their brothers and fathers to be able to carry out one kind of task while they become skilled at another. As time passes, it is hard for girls to catch up on the years of tinkering and learning what goes where that has been shared between father and son, man to man. Some girls do develop these so-called masculine interests, but most do not. The divide between masculine and feminine interests – the traditional pursuits of boys and girls – is naturally passed on from one generation to the next. Even today.

It is this and attitudes towards the acceptable behaviour of little girls that form the basis for the invisible woman trying to be the perfect mother. The invisibility of household and nurturing skills, which cannot be transformed into a trade in the way that motor mechanics can be, contribute to society's failure to appreciate the traditional role of women, even in the home. Yet this is often the role that our daughters are raised to fulfil in order to take their honourable place within the family club.

Beverley's story: the good daughter

This path to invisibility is all too clear in the story of 10-year-old Beverley, who was brought to see me by her mother Joan. Every morning, when it was time to leave for school, Beverley had wept and screamed, begging her mother not to make her go. Finally, six weeks before, she had stopped attending school altogether. Joan was concerned for her daughter and wanted to find out if there was anything she could do to help.

I saw them together in an effort to get the full family picture. When we had set up the appointment, I had asked if Beverley's father Ben could come too, but I was told that he couldn't get away from work. It quickly became clear that he had little to do with raising his daughter. That was the mother's role.

"I don't know why Beverley doesn't want to go to school," said Joan. "She makes friends easily and does really well at her school work. At home she seems quiet and content. We are really close and spend a lot of time together.

"She helps me a lot with her little brother Luke. He is Beverley's youngest brother, of course. Ben and I also have two older sons who work for him in our business. They all spend a lot of time working. We have done really well for ourselves. We started with nothing, but now we have a successful family business."

I asked about Joan's role in the family.

"I keep the house going. I used to help with the business, but once the little one, Luke, came along, I stopped. I want to be with him and give him the best start in life. One after the other, the boys joined their father straight from school. I have Beverley to look after still, of course. She helps me so much around the house and with Luke, too."

As the story of the family unfolded, it became obvious that all its members lived and worked together. The older sons left school and went to work for their father. Beverley, who was about eight years younger than her next oldest brother, was the ideal and only daughter. She was seen by everyone as the companion her mother needed. Joan now had a daughter to share things with and to talk to. She raised Beverley as a carbon copy of herself, giving her all the skills to care for her older brothers and her father and now little brother Luke.

How was Beverley reacting to this? Within this family, her role was to serve and have no needs of her own. Even the request to me to help Beverley overcome her reluctance to attend school was suspect when her mother revealed that "Without Beverley around at home, I don't know what I'd do with myself. She helps me so much by looking after Luke. They adore each other, you know. I thought there might be a little jealousy there, but it's the opposite. She spends all her time looking after Luke."

How could Beverley assert her own needs? The anxiety attacks she had as she left home for school could be seen as her way of expressing her developing fear of going out into the world. After all, in this family Beverley is now the only person who has to "go out" into the world. Her older brothers and father work in the family business. Mother and baby Luke are at home. If Beverley's destiny in the family club is to care for the men and the babies, why did she have to "go out" and learn? The contrast Beverley experiences between the outside world and her family life is too great for her young mind to handle. She is beginning to want things for herself, and having that available "outside" – at school, with friends – is such a contrast to the family club that it is easier for her to choose to stay at home and become a full member of the family club. It may also be easier for Beverley to be close to Luke and to care for him than to be jealous of him and so feel the disapproval of the family club. At least if she becomes caring and "maternal", her behaviour is accepted and even praised.

If Beverley chooses to go out into the world, what will she do to the other members of the family club? If she pursues her own needs, she will challenge the role her mother has taken, to serve others and be a perfect mother. If she pursues her own needs, she will be seen as not supporting the family business, not supporting her brothers and the rest of the family. If she pursues her own needs, she might be responsible for her mother's likely "breakdown" when Joan is left with no companion or help in caring for Luke and the others.

By having anxiety attacks, Beverley is revealing the conflict within her the only way she can. In addition, her own parents and brothers are unconsciously encouraging her to stay within the safety of the family club.

We might also assume that going to school may have become a conflict for Beverley because there she would see boys and girls being treated as equals, with no one gender being invisible. But as we shall see, this can be the wrong assumption.

Ignoring a girl's feelings

Even in the United States where, in the eyes of the rest of the world, the sexes are treated more equally than elsewhere, a 10-year-old girl was invisible within her own school. LaShonda

Davis complained to her teachers and later to the principal of her school that a fellow male pupil was grabbing at her breasts and crotch and threatening to have sex with her. This lasted for six months and no action was taken; the two children were kept sitting next to each other in class. LaShonda finally told her mother of her problems, and then mother and daughter went to a lawyer. In January 1999, the US Supreme Court ruled that the school LaShonda attended was liable for sexual harassment.[7]

I think that LaShonda's complaints were ignored because she was a little girl complaining about sexual advances – her teachers refused to see the sexuality in the "children" in their care. This is rather like the father who will not accept his daughter's growing sexual maturity. LaShonda became invisible because her complaints were not seen as important to anyone else. As a girl, her emotional upset was not valued or taken notice of because she was being raised by society to be a carer of others – a perfect mother. If LaShonda had hit her male classmate and bloodied his nose, she would not have been invisible. Quite the opposite: I suspect that the full force of the school's disciplinary system would have come to bear on her.

Girls are groomed to be good wives and mothers. They are expected to consider others and to show a tolerance even for inappropriate behaviour. Complaints about mistreatment or feeling bad are dismissed if they interfere with the values of the family club. The rules of the club for girls are often simple: think of others before yourself – later you will need this experience if you are to be a perfect mother.

The teenage years: training for motherhood

What happens to girls who act like girls?

Little girls grow older. They develop their own interests and ideas, and some of these come from influences outside the family club, such as school friends and the fashion and music industries. Their interests change from those of little girls to those of developing young women. As they begin to form their own sense of self, those around them find this break with their previous passive development difficult if not threatening.

"I just can't stop myself. When she goes out shopping for clothes, she doesn't want the nice dress I'd like her to wear at our next family gathering. No, she wants the short leather skirt and the little black top. I say 'no' – of course, she sulks and so, in the end, we don't get anything."

George's daughter Michelle is nine years old and already being influenced by the fashion industry – just as girls are supposed to be influenced. Parents will probably always lament how young their children are when they start to have minds of their own with the opinions to go with them. Nothing really changes. Their own parents lamented the same life stages.

George's daughter is becoming a woman, as society expects her to become. But at the same time, her parents and society condemn her new choices.

"How can she be my little girl and dress like that? That isn't how I expected a daughter of mine, only nine years old, to dress. What would everyone think if she went out like that? I can't believe that some of her friends are already allowed to be like that."

What does George mean by "like that"? Michelle is still a girl but trying out her new-found sense of self. She is beginning to separate from her parents, to go out to parties where her parents do not stay with her, to be drawn into the teen culture of pop idols and female sexuality. At nine, Michelle is becoming aware of the power she holds over boys and men, but she is also vulnerable to the control they have over how she is expected to behave.

It is this new sexuality that makes George uncomfortable. Michelle is becoming a young woman, but George wants his pure, innocent, obedient little girl back and so attempts to exert his control over her. He is trying to preserve everything within the family club but allow for the inevitable changes within Michelle. He knows that it is impossible to stop her from growing up, so he makes it clear that he will accept her only as long as she is a good girl, a model daughter and a good, caring woman.

Does this sound extreme? While not many parents will admit openly that they are upset by their daughters' new choices, most do struggle with them. Girls are seen as vulnerable, passive, in need of protection from the ugly outside world and even uglier teenage boys – the same teenage boys from the same family groups that protect the girls.

This makes sense only if we accept that boys and girls have been raised with different sets of behaviour and expectations. If boys are "sullen", this is interpreted as "angry active", while if their sisters show the same signs, they are described as "sulking passive". The boys, encouraged in their pursuits, are expected to go out and get what they want. The tougher they dress, the more masculine they act, the more proud of them their parents, and especially their fathers, tend to be.

It seems that fathers are often the key, whether part of a two-parent family or parents living apart. Over and over again in the therapy room, I have heard mothers say how difficult it is for their husbands to accept that their daughters want to go out, to dress according to their own taste, to have a boyfriend. At the same time, fathers say how hard they find the transition from little girl to youthful adolescent in their daughters. Sons simply do not produce the same concern.

Daughters are supposed to remain asexual – without sex. However, compared with their brothers, they mature and become aware of their sexual power earlier. Some daughters find that acting immaturely with their fathers works for them. If they want a favour, they act like little girls. But if they want something for themselves, some independence or that leather skirt, they often have to endure the disapproval of their fathers. The message is clear: behave and please the man of the house and you will be rewarded; be yourself and explore your new-found self and you will be meet with disapproval.

Good daughters remain "feminine", in the traditional meaning of the word. They continue to help around the house and even care for younger brothers and sisters. In some households – more than you would think – daughters look after their older brothers, cooking and washing for the family if the mother is away or too busy to cope. The mothers of these good daughters encourage this behaviour, often in the guise of "sharing chores" or "spending time together". It is also the mothers who are the vanguards of good behaviour and good language in their daughters. Good daughters become a part of the family rather than individuals in their own right. Good daughters become invisible.

It is also at this age – the approach of adolescence – that good girls develop a range of psychosomatic illnesses. These are illnesses that are recognized as strongly influenced by stress and emotion. Headaches, stomach pains, asthma and menstrual difficulties are all examples of illnesses commonly influenced by a person's psychological health. This does not mean that the illnesses are not "real", but rather that their severity varies with mood. It has been suggested that having to conform – or, rather, the struggle between wanting to achieve for oneself and the inability to see any way of doing so without receiving the disapproval of society and especially the family – leads to these illnesses.[8] The intelligent, ambitious daughter is presented with the reality of her own mother, often also intelligent and previously ambitious, who has abandoned her own plans in order to raise a family – a great contrast to the apparently successful father who has not had to compromise his goals. This may not be an accurate picture of the choices made within the parental partnership, but it is how it may appear to the daughter.

The messages, often a mix of the spoken and unspoken, are clear but contradictory:

- A woman achieves nothing as her role as mother and home-maker is valueless.

  versus

- A woman's true role is to be a mother. This is her greatest fulfilment.

These conflicting messages create a conflict within the susceptible daughter. If she begins to achieve too much outside the home – in sports, education or at work – she becomes sick so that she once again becomes dependent on her parents or boyfriend/husband. Once dependent, she reconciles herself to the good wife and mother role, abandoning her own plans for independence – which, in turn, causes the internal struggle perpetuating the asthma, eating disorder, migraine or some other illness.

What happens to girls who behave like one of the boys?

Parents' reactions to daughters who are active, loud and even "aggressive" are likely to be more harsh, more controlling or more despairing than their reactions to the same behaviours in sons. Parents, and particularly mothers, appear with far more frequency in the therapy room asking for help for way-ward daughters than for wayward sons. If a mother seeks help with coping with a son, it is often in response to her discovery that he is taking drugs, in trouble with the police or involved in some other behaviour causing concern. It takes a serious, law-breaking or life-threatening event for mothers to seek help with their sons. It takes far less to evoke concern and the seeking of help for daughters. Disobedience, using "bad language", dressing the "wrong way", having a series of boyfriends, starting a sexual relationship or returning home late from evenings out with friends will cause enough worry and concern for mothers to look for help.

It seems odd that, while it is often the father who objects to the growing sexual maturity of his little girl, it is the mother who seeks help for the wayward daughter. On closer examination, I have found that the father has often washed his hands of the affair once this wayward, independent behaviour has become established in his daughter. He will no longer have anything to do with her and instead directs all his objections and complaints to his wife. It is the good wife and mother who shoulders all the strain. It is the good wife and mother who seeks help, as much for herself as for her daughter. The good wife and mother becomes the mediator between daughter and father without any opinion of her own. The good wife and mother has become invisible. The daughter has become "a problem". The father is "right".

The daughter who stays out late worries her parents, who assume that "the worst" has happened. Their concerns centre around the risks of her keeping company with boys. If her brother is out late, they are also concerned that he is out with the boys, his friends, but their main worries about him centre around rowdy behaviour – sex does not come into it. This is a reflection of the relative lack of consequences of sex for boys, of their tendency to regard sex as recreational. Girls, on the other hand, are not supposed to see sex as anything casual.

Even if the family no longer demands marriage before sex, they do expect serious, monogamous relationships for their daughters.

This, of course, reflects the consequences of sexual intimacy for girls. The fear of an unplanned pregnancy is very real for these parents. They hope that ultimately their daughters will become perfect mothers, but see this as possible only in a monogamous, marital relationship. They make the automatic assumption that a single mother will be a bad mother; the idea of single motherhood does not fit in with the rules of the family club.

The conflict faced by young women is contained in the dual messages sent by both the media and the family:

- You can have it all.

  versus

- If you want to be happy, you should behave and conform.

The media image of a young woman is either someone who is married with children, happy and content, or someone who is single and having relationship difficulties. If a teenage girl does not conform and show the caring, self-sacrificing behaviour expected of good women and perfect mothers, the family begins to worry about what will happen to her. Will she develop into a bad woman, one who is aggressive, troublesome, promiscuous and, worse, a bad mother or not even a mother at all? There is no thought given to the choice of a young woman to be single, career orientated, childless and happy. This choice, available to young men, is seen in girls only in terms of a failure to form a relationship or be happy.

The goal of most families for their daughters is to see them settled down, married and with children. It is their "biological destiny". Since this is what normal girls do, family members will encourage this behaviour above all others. After all, this is what their mothers did and they regard themselves as normal. The father chose a wife who was prepared to become a mother, so both parents see parenthood and especially motherhood as the highest calling for girls. After all, this is what normal women do.

6

Pregnancy and preparation for motherhood

Women are prepared for motherhood. This preparation intensifies during pregnancy when, in everyone's mind, the focus of attention changes from the woman to her unborn child.

Catherine becomes invisible

Catherine walked into the bar and ordered a drink. She looked around to find an empty seat and, seeing one over by the window, sat down. The place was fairly full with lunchtime drinkers, men and women taking a break from the office. Eyes turned to look at her. Catherine could see some people motioning to where she was sitting and speaking in hushed tones.

Carefully Catherine took out her cigarettes and pulled one from the pack. She asked a woman sitting nearby if she had a light. The woman turned and looked Catherine up and down. Settling her eyes on the pregnant bulge, she removed the cigarette from her mouth and said, "No," before turning back to her friends. Catherine couldn't miss the disapproval emanating from the woman. She felt the group looking at her as she fumbled in her own bag to find her lighter. She had been prepared for some reaction, but already she felt more than a little uncomfortable.

As she lit her own cigarette, another woman walked over from the bar and stood in front of her. "How could you hurt your baby this way?" she demanded.

The man with her joined in: "Don't you know how much you are hurting your baby? You are making your baby smoke that cigarette . . . and drink that beer."

Catherine felt cornered. She had never been spoken to with such animosity before. Perhaps this experiment was going to be harder than she thought. She had expected reactions from others when she had planned to drink and smoke while appearing pregnant, but not to this extent. Her university professor had thought the idea of going into a bar with a pillow stuffed inside her loose clothing was an interesting concept. He had warned her that she might be criticized, but neither of them had predicted this open hostility.

What is it about a pregnant woman that changes people's behaviour so much? The presence of the baby inside the woman suddenly seems to allow others to believe that the woman herself is public property, open to scrutiny. The people who made comments to Catherine did not consider what she might want for herself or what her decisions for her baby might be. Instead, her needs and desires became secondary at best. However, I would suggest that it is worse than even this: Catherine had become invisible as a human being.

What happens to women like Catherine when they become mothers? If the pregnancy is welcome, the first feelings are often of embarking on a new stage of life. Friends and family offer their congratulations and tell the woman how wonderful it all is, how pleased they are. The couple is offered words of support and encouragement. Well, that is the storybook version anyway! In reality, many women find the first weeks and months difficult as the full impact of what is about to happen strikes them.

Why is it that so many women actually feel desperately unhappy at this time? Hormones? Any weepiness is usually put down to hormones and changes in the body. Any concerns or reservations are dismissed as "natural" rather than discussed seriously. At the very point at which a woman fulfils what many see as her biological destiny, any emotional reaction is dismissed as if it belongs to an unstable child.

However, to the woman, she has become a mother-to-be rather than the woman she is and was. There is a sudden realization that she is no longer free to choose just for herself, that life will never be the same again. It is now that it becomes obvious that, even with a loving supportive partner, it is the woman, the perfect mother, who actually carries the baby. As plans are made to receive medical care and organize maternity leave, the reality of the changes begin to break through the initial elation. The conflict between how the woman actually feels and the idealized image of the perfect mother is hard to cope with – especially the first time.

Induction into the motherhood club

The difficulties faced by mothers because of their sudden invisibility are graphically described by Bonnie and Ann in the following exchange of e-mails from the CompuServe Family Services Forum on the Internet.[9]

Subj: stomach touching   **Section**: Pregnancy/Birth

To: all   05 May 1999 04:18:11

From: Bonnie P

How do you get people to stop "touching" your stomach when they find out that you're pregnant? I had this problem with my first pregnancy, and never knew how to handle it. I didn't want to hurt anyone's feelings, yet I really feel as if my "personal space" is invaded when other people (even close friends) pat my belly. They usually do it so spontaneously that I'm left quite surprised and speechless. Still, I would love to be able to say something to them that's tactful, gets the point across (that they shouldn't do it again), and doesn't hurt their feelings.

Any suggestions?

Subj: stomach touching **Section**: Pregnancy/Birth
To: Bonnie P 05 May 1999 15:14:14
From: Ann O

I've had this happen to me throughout all three of my pregnancies. People I know didn't bother me as much, but when strangers in the grocery store, school, movies, etc. did it, it drove me crazy. I decided to touch the person back on their tummy whenever they touched me. The look on their faces was priceless.

When talking with each other, pregnant women often confide their deep-seated fears and resentment of what is happening to them. However, only snippets of truth are allowed out at any one time. No one talks about all the changes a woman has to face when pregnant. The physical changes are bad enough – the feelings of bloatedness, tender breasts and nipples that seem to have taken on lives of their own, and the morning sickness that seems to last all day. After the initial elation of finding themselves pregnant, many women agree that they would gladly return to their "pre-pregnant" days.

These women become mothers from the moment of conception (or preconception if they take advice regarding diet, drink, drugs and fertility), and they will remain mothers until the moment of death of either themselves or their children.

Watch the *Jerry Springer Show* when there is a pregnant woman on stage. As commonly happens on this programme, everyone around her is expected to be violent. But the pregnant woman is expected to be demure and unemotional. If someone hits out at her, they are admonished for hitting a "pregnant woman", but if she hits out, she is criticized: "You're carrying a child. You can't do that."

The woman herself has become invisible. It is an abrupt process, occurring over a period of just a few months. The medicalization of pregnancy adds to the process. The woman hands over her body to be probed and prodded by doctors and and other medical staff. The focus of attention turns to the unborn child. The terms "prenatal care" or "antenatal care" even emphasize the existence of the child rather than the pregnant woman. Her needs, her wants, her intellect and her abilities are now secondary to every need of the unborn child inside her. The treatment she receives as the pregnancy progresses simply serves to prepare her further to remain invisible after the birth.

A woman who is automatically given medical checks – such as an internal pelvic examination or testing her blood sugar levels – which previously she would have expected to have had explained and her permission sought, is curtly told that the baby needs to be checked. What can she say? "I don't want you to do this" sounds as if she doesn't care about her unborn child, which is, of course, unthinkable. Any concerns or objections concerning what is being done to her become too difficult to voice. The woman is trapped into being the perfect mother-to-be – silent and invisible.

The process continues with the marketing of childbirth and early motherhood. The woman buys pregnancy books that address the changes in her body and even some of her worries. However, the main thrust of these books is how to look after yourself so that the *baby* thrives and, just as importantly, how to ensure that the new father is taken care of. There are warnings about how he may feel jealous and left out once the baby arrives, accompanied by advice on how to avoid this. Many books on the market advise us on how to be perfect mothers, what to do for our children, how to keep our man and even how to be a working mother. When these books acknowledge the needs of the woman herself at all, they are relegated to the end, after all the other demands on her.

The pregnant woman is responsible for everything. To be the perfect mother-to-be, she must be serene yet strong. She must be considerate of others and yet look after herself so that the baby will thrive. Medical studies, gleefully reported in the press[10], claim that even being anxious can adversely affect the foetus, the effects being directly compared with the harm mothers-to-be do when they smoke. Once again, the responsibility for all the difficulties is placed on the mother. The perfect mother-to-be is being prepared to feel guilt and to be invisible in the presence of her future child's needs.

The day of the birth arrives and the medical procedure takes over. The birth plan, which describes the way the mother wants the delivery to be, is all in place at the hospital. However, most women have tales to tell of not being listened to or of feeling completely unimportant in the birthing process. They become passive recipients of medical care.

The new mother has joined another exclusive club: the motherhood club. Non-mothers are never given the secret information about pregnancy, birth and the realities of being a mother. Non-mothers do not receive a snip-by-snip account of the episiotomy or a drip-by-drip description of flooding breasts. The after-effects of birth are hidden from those not initiated into this exclusive club. The stinging reality of peeing over stitches or trying to open your bowels when you're afraid that everything will tear apart are closely guarded secrets.

So here is the woman, faced with a small bundle of baby just when she has gone through the most harrowing, strenuous experience of her lifetime. "Love at first sight" – that's how it is supposed to be. How is a woman to cope with all these expectations? The truth is – she can't. However, if she were to whisper, even to herself, a word about it not being what everyone else seems to think, she would not be a perfect mother. Once again, the new mother is trapped in the image of what it is to be a perfect mother, with her true feelings and thoughts kept invisible as she and everyone else in the family celebrate the arrival of the newest member.

The inner conflicts between the truth and the social and emotional pressures the woman has to contend with are buried inside . . . until they surface in depression. The labels may vary – postnatal depression, depression, anxiety – but they are often heard at this time. This is not the classic "hormonal imbalance depression" that starts within days of birth. This depression grows slowly over weeks and months as the conflicts within the woman rage. The catch is that she may not recognize that she is experiencing conflicts; instead, she may believe that she is a failure, unable to cope with what she believes is the most natural thing in the world: motherhood. If she does recognize the conflicts within, she may feel completely trapped, unable to change things for the better and still remain a perfect mother to her child.

This is the cost of becoming the icon of the perfect mother. It is time to replace this with a new, more forgiving image: the adult mother.

7

Perfect mothers: balancing the extended family

Perfect mothers hold the family together. This is one of those absolute truths we do not question. Instead we act on this truth blindly, feeling obliged to host the family Christmas dinner or throw a children's birthday party that will include grandparents, aunts and uncles. Some of us go as far as holding two birthday parties when the children are small – one for the child and all his or her friends and then a family gathering – so that no one is left out of the celebration. Or we hold our own child's birthday party at the grandparents' house because they will feel rejected if we turn down their offer. We keep the family club going without consideration for our own needs. Other mothers look on in wonder at the perfect mother who is always so good to her children and the rest of her family.

Anne's story

Every Friday afternoon, the telephone rings. Every Friday afternoon, Anne becomes more tense as the time approaches. Sometimes it is three o'clock, sometimes four, but the phone always rings. Anne dreads that call. It is from her mother-in-law Brenda.

Anne knows that Brenda is filling in her weekly diary, her list of social events. Anne and the children are always included. Brenda calls to arrange a convenient time to come over for lunch. Sometimes Brenda invites Anne to visit, but usually Brenda comes to Anne. In the past, Anne found that the stress of cleaning up the children, putting the high chair into the car and carrying all the young ones' paraphernalia was too much. Although the days of bottles and high chairs are long gone, the pattern has remained. The phone call heralds another lunch, prepared and cooked by Anne, but always initiated by Brenda. Not that Brenda ever comes if Anne is at home alone. The visit has to include the children, Anne's two sons.

Brenda thinks the world of the boys. She is the perfect grandmother – coming to visit every week, bringing sweets and small toys. The sweets were a bone of contention at the beginning. Anne was feeding her sons lots of vegetables and fruit, with a little meat, and following all the advice given to mothers about giving children nutritious meals and avoiding tooth decay. Anne would spend ages looking for sugar-free, colour-free, additive-free drinks for her sons, and then Brenda would visit and give them small paper bags containing a selection of mixed sweets. Anne tried to stop her but Brenda was adamant: "It's just a small bag. It won't hurt. What does it matter, once a week? They're only little children once, you know." Anne's opinion obviously did not count.

Every week, Anne listens to stories about when her husband Thomas was a small boy. Thomas was such a perfect child. Even the stories about him being "bad" seem to involve the most minor of misdemeanours. As her own boys have grown, Anne has seen the "tut" of disapproval cross Brenda's face as they come in dirty from playing in the nearby fields.

For some reason, Brenda doesn't demand that Thomas be at the weekly lunches. In fact, Anne has noticed that Thomas avoids being home whenever his mother visits, even if he is free.

Anne knows that Thomas will do anything rather than say "no" to his mother – anything, that is, except socialize with her. He sees her a few times a year at most. He will speak with her on the phone on Sundays but never involves himself in arranging the weekly meeting – after all, he won't be coming to it. Thomas has always felt pleased that his mother and Anne get along so well that they lunch together every week.

The harmonious extended family has survived because Anne has held it together. But she hates the weekly phone call. She feels she is being slotted in between the hairdresser and a coffee morning with a church group. However, saying "no" causes ill feeling and then Brenda complains to Thomas.

Anne feels that, in Brenda's eyes, she is invisible or, worse, a bad mother. It is as if she does not count, does not even exist in this world where her husband was such a perfect child and her sons should receive everything. In her mother-in-law's eyes, nothing is too much for any of them.

The cost of being a perfect mother to the whole family

Anne has always wanted to be a perfect mother. She has two young children, a nice home, a good husband and lots of loving relatives. This is how it appears on the surface. But the cost of this dream family has been high. Anne feels desperately low and overwhelmed. At the same time, she feels that she has no reason to be unhappy. Like Julie in Chapter 2, she thinks that she has everything she could wish for. And like Julie, others have envied her the leisurely lifestyle of "the stay-at-home perfect mother". This has made it even harder for Anne to speak of her unhappiness and extreme tiredness. If she voices any resentment at caring for others, it seems the height of selfishness.

Whatever her children want or need, they get. Anne is up before them in the morning and goes to bed late at night. There never seem enough hours in the day to do the shopping and the school runs, care for the youngest boy, help with homework, prepare food and still be there for her husband when he wants to talk. Then there is her mother- in-law. Brenda always seems to find something to raise her eyebrows about. If she sees dust on the living-room bookcase, she will wipe it with her finger. Anne doesn't know which is worse – for nothing to be said or for Brenda to ask for a duster! Whichever it is, Anne is left feeling that she is a failure as a wife and as a mother.

As for Anne's own life – she isn't sure that she has one any more. She can't remember the last time she had a day out by herself. She and Thomas have not been away for a night in a hotel since their first son was born seven years ago. A few years before, she had thought of returning to work but Thomas had persuaded her to wait until the children were older. All of Anne's energies are involved in the care of others. She tries to keep things as they should be and everyone happy, and all she wants in return is to feel good about herself. Now she is beginning to realize that the more she tries to be the perfect mother, the less good she feels about herself.

Anne has become invisible because she is the perfect mother. Her opinions and choices, such as not feeding the children sweets, are dismissed as unimportant by Brenda. Anne is nice, quiet and compliant – and ignored. Insisting that her opinions are heard and taken notice of by others would not fit with the image of the perfect mother. But insisting on being taken notice of as a woman and the mother of children would be the action of an adult mother.

Time for Anne to change

Anne told me her story. She had come to therapy because she felt stuck. She felt unable to change what was happening but, at the same time, did not wish to upset anybody. The extra tension caused by her mother-in-law had become unbearable, and she knew she needed help in coping. We talked some more.

"So what happens if you don't spend time and energy making sure you're home when your mother-in-law comes to visit?"

"I don't know what would happen. I imagine Brenda would complain about me to Thomas."

"So what will Thomas do then?"

"I don't know . . . I suppose he'll moan at me."

"How can you deal with this?"

Finally Anne rebelled. She did not come right out and tell Brenda that she did not want to see her. She did not feel brave enough. Instead, when Brenda tried to arrange her visit, she started to say that she was busy. Then, every couple of weeks or so, she would say that the boys were out or that she had made arrangements to take them somewhere or even that she was visiting friends of her own. Although this made the phone calls stressful, it gave Anne a series of Brenda-less weeks – not having to clean up the house, not having to think of what meal to prepare. Anne felt triumphant and talked of how good it was not to have to spend time with Brenda.

Avoiding having to say a categorical "no" is not unusual. It takes much courage and confidence to change patterns that have been established for years or even generations. But to make changes for the better, this eventually has to be done.

For Anne, the time to change came the day when Thomas returned home from work and asked why she hadn't seen his mother. Anne was prepared.

As calmly as she could, she told him that she was tired of always having to be available. She explained how she felt about Brenda and her belief that the visits were to see the children, not her. She spoke of how it was she who had to cook a meal, clean up and so on. Thomas listened and agreed with Anne, but then talked of how hurt his mother was. Brenda had called him at work, crying over the phone, feeling left out. This was what Anne had predicted, but she had not prepared herself for Thomas's reaction, which was to plead with Anne to see his mother so that he wouldn't have to deal with Brenda's telephone calls at work.

Anne came to her next session very down. She described her feelings: "I feel completely powerless. I felt better . . . you know I did when I didn't have to see Brenda . . . but now I'm stuck between Thomas and his mother. You see, he's begged me to see her. He can't stand having her cry. He's always been that way. He can't bear me getting upset. If I get tearful, he just shuts off. I've had to learn not to be emotional over any-thing. But his mother does this every time. She bursts into tears over the phone and he instantly agrees to what she wants just to shut her up."

Anne began to sound less flat and more angry as she went on: "So here I am again, doing something I don't want to do. It was just the same when we got married, you know. I wanted a quiet wedding and my parents were happy with that, too. But that wasn't good enough for Thomas's mother. She made such a fuss about all these distant relatives and how she'd always wanted Thomas to have a big wedding that, in the end, we went along with it to keep her quiet. We've been doing the same thing ever since. I just can't face upsetting Thomas."

Anne described how, time after time, Brenda had got her own way by pushing Thomas.

"How do you feel about Thomas asking you to do something you don't want to do?" I asked.

Anne looked surprised at the directness of my question. There was a moment's silence and then she smiled slightly.

"You're right. He's pushing me into seeing Brenda. But what do I do? If I don't see Brenda, then she phones Thomas at work and then he pushes me to see her."

"Why does he push you to see Brenda?"

"Because he can't stand the crying – I told you. He can't say 'no' to her."

"So what I'm hearing is that, because Thomas can't say 'no' to his mother, then you can't either."

"Yes, that's right."

Anne hands the problem back to her husband

Anne is acting as a go-between for Brenda and Thomas. Thomas sees his mother only when he absolutely has to – Christmas and birthdays – but hides this by encouraging contact between Brenda, Anne and his sons. At the same time, when Brenda telephones and cries, saying that she wants to see more of Anne, she is demonstrating two things: her need to have contact with Thomas and her knowledge of how, in the past, her crying has always made him do what she wants. The pattern of Anne acting as the buffer between Thomas and his mother started before their marriage. Because Anne did not want to upset Thomas, she went along with the changes to their wedding plans. Then, because she did not want to make Thomas angry, she was faced with having to see Brenda once a week.

Anne and I talked about this further and came to the conclusion that the problem did not belong to Anne. It belonged to Thomas and his mother. Anne was being used to maintain the status quo between them. This suited the family club, which does not like change. But by doing this, Anne was actually preventing the changes that needed to occur between Thomas and his mother.

We spent the rest of the session talking about how Anne could change her own part in this family club behaviour. Anne was tempted to return to the way things had been and see Brenda again rather than upset Thomas. But she had come to see that, if that happened, her mother-in-law would continue to rule Thomas and, through Thomas, her for the rest of their lives. Anne had to take responsibility for herself, for what she wanted, and leave Thomas and Brenda to settle their own relationship.

Anne went home, and on Friday came the usual telephone call. Brenda obviously expected things to be easy for her since Thomas had agreed to talk with Anne. So she was very surprised when Anne told her that she would like to meet her for lunch at a local restaurant, without the children. Brenda was obviously flustered but agreed.

They met a few days later. Anne was nervous but felt surprisingly in control. She noticed immediately that Brenda was very uncomfortable. She didn't like this change in routine, and being in public meant open displays of emotion had to be controlled.

Anne started by telling Brenda what she thought were the good things about their relationship. Then she acknowledged that she had not seen her much recently. "I expect you've been wondering why. I know you telephoned Thomas at work to talk to him about it."

Brenda was surprised at this. She had obviously assumed that Thomas would keep his talks with his own mother a secret.

Anne went on. Now that the children were older, she said, she was busier doing things for herself and her time was no longer tied so closely to the boys or the house. She also stated that she knew that Brenda really wanted to see Thomas and the children rather than spending time with her. Although Brenda offered reassurances and denials, Anne could see that her point had been made.

She moved on to address the main question. She commented that Brenda must miss Thomas as she really did not see him very much. Brenda was surprised that someone else had recognized this need. Anne refused to be drawn into "arranging" anything between Thomas and Brenda, and made it clear that arrangements to visit her at home needed to be made with her direct. They had nothing to do with Thomas. Anne had stepped outside the family club.

The message left with Brenda was clear. Anne was a woman in her own right. She was Thomas's wife. She was the mother of the two grandchildren. But she was also Anne, who had a life of her own. If Brenda wanted something involving Anne, she needed to arrange it with Anne. Anne was an adult and was allowed to say "no".

Of course this was only the first step. Old patterns of behaviour continue in others even if you change your own.

Later the same afternoon, Brenda telephoned Thomas, complaining about Anne and crying. Thomas came home tense and annoyed with Anne, but this time she was ready. She repeated to Thomas what she had said to Brenda and told him clearly that any meetings between Anne and Brenda were for her to arrange or to refuse, and if Brenda telephoned him at work to complain or cry, it wouldn't change her decision. She even suggested that Thomas should tell Brenda not to ring him at work about personal upsets.

Thomas was annoyed and stressed, but Anne did not lose track of her message. She was saying clearly what it was that she wanted. If Thomas did not like what Brenda did on the phone, he should deal with it. He needed to recognize Anne's right to choose whether she saw Brenda or not. She also made it clear that, in return, she would see Brenda sometimes because she was, after all, Thomas's mother.

Anne had returned the problem to the people to whom it belonged – Brenda and Thomas. For years, she had played the perfect mother and held the family together by taking responsibility for other people's tensions. Why had Anne done this? Because she was the perfect example of the perfect mother. She stayed at home caring for her children, sat on school committees, did a little charity work and had a life that revolved around her family.

Changing into an adult mother

For women like Anne, "family" can come to include all the relatives from both sides. Those perfect mothers who remain at home with their children are seen as having no other role than to care for others. The perfect mother has no separate rights or feelings of her own. She is there to serve the family, to never say "no". And women such as Anne find it hard to say "no" because of the guilt they feel by not fulfilling their role in their family club. The perfect mothers hold their families together, becoming overwhelmed with problems that belong to others or that at least should be shared.

The adult mother is going to be seen as difficult and selfish, compared with the perfect mother. As Anne began to look at her difficulties with Brenda, she stopped doing what she had done for years – being the perfect mother to the entire family. She worked towards becoming an adult mother. She stopped taking on problems that were not hers and began to say "no" without overwhelming feelings of guilt.

Summary of Anne's difficulties and solutions

Anne was trying to cope with pressures from many sources.

- She felt her needs did not count or were dismissed by others.
- She was expected to look after her children and other members of the family before herself at all times.
- She felt invisible.
- Change seemed impossible as trying to say "no" caused arguments with Thomas or tears from Brenda.
- Everyone else was happy, so why wasn't she?

These are some of the changes Anne made.

- She started to talk about what she did not like.
- She told her husband that she would not take on his problem with his mother.
- She talked with Brenda and then stepped away from acting as a go-between.
- She started to think about herself!

To help you think about your own role in your family club and whose problems you may be solving without realizing it, look at Part Two.

8

What happens when nothing changes

Many perfect mothers believe that their turn will come when their children are grown. In the meantime, these women focus all their energies on them as they grow and support them through their adolescence. They act as taxi drivers and teachers for homework, provide money for school trips and nights out, cook endless amounts of food and provide local accommodation to their friends – all in the name of being loving supportive mothers.

For some children, this goes too far and they find they can use and abuse their parents. These are the teenagers who, smothered with love, suffer no consequences if they don't come home at the agreed time, if they get into trouble at school or even if they break the law by drinking and driving. The perfect mother always understands why it is so hard for her son or daughter and makes excuses for what is actually inconsiderate or bad behaviour. This type of perfect mother is often allied more closely to her children than to her partner, and when the partner tries to impose some order and consequences, the mother intercedes and prevents any change. The tension between the couple rises, causing its own problems when, in fact, the problem truly belongs to the rebellious teenager.

As the age at which the children will leave home approaches, the perfect mother begins to look outwards. If she has not worked away from home for many years, the possibility of getting a small part-time job might be considered as a means of re-entering the world of work. Or she may decide to continue to focus on the home but take time for herself and her partner. Whether she goes out to work or remains at home, this is the new lease of life she has long promised herself. She dreams of weekends spent in hide-away cottages or out-of-the-way hotels and long evenings shared with her partner. But the dreams are often not matched by the reality.

When the children leave home: Dorothy's story

Dorothy came to see me after a doctor's appointment. She had been feeling very low for weeks. She described herself, her life and her family. She was married to a man she cared about very much, and they had two daughters who had now left home to lead lives of their own. Dorothy was also close to her parents, although this relationship had begun to change recently as they became older and more needy.

Dorothy proceeded to tell me about her daughters, of whom she was very proud. They had been so close, Dorothy and the girls, and she missed them very much. They had been the centre of her life. But at the same time, she had looked forward to having time to meet friends, revive her old hobby of writing poetry and, most of all, spend much-needed time with her husband. However, none of this seemed to have happened, and as the weeks had turned into months since the last daughter had left home, Dorothy had become more and more depressed.

When things stay the same because no one else is affected the way you are

"I thought that, once the children had left home, we would

have more time for each other, to share things. Instead he has no time for me because of his job."

Dorothy's husband Henry not only had a demanding job but, she told me, he was also a sociable man and was often out and about with business colleagues. He had spent the previous 20 years working hard on his career, while Dorothy had focused on raising their children. He knew she had done a good job and was proud of his daughters. He didn't understand why Dorothy was now so low and withdrawn.

I suspected that he had carried on with his life as it had been for the past two decades without it occurring to him that there was a need to do anything differently. After all, this was his role. When Dorothy became upset and tearful in the evenings after he returned home from work, he could not understand why she felt that way. He would suggest that she visit one of their friends or start writing again, just like she had talked about for so many years, but his suggestions didn't seem to get anywhere. Henry reassured himself with the thought that at least Dorothy had her parents to talk to every day.

When children are replaced by others in need

In her husband's mind, Dorothy's parents seemed to have taken the place of their daughters. Perhaps this would help her through this rough patch.

But Dorothy's view of her life was very different: "Even when I do have some time, my parents need something. I go round to see them most days, but it never seems to be enough for them. My father complains constantly and I hate to upset him. They won't do anything for themselves any more. I tried to explain this to the doctor when I saw him, but he told me how lucky I was that they lived nearby and how wonderful it was to have such a close-knit family nowadays."

Far from comforting Dorothy, her parents were partly responsible for her unhappiness. She was faced with a conflict that is commonly experienced by perfect mothers: the perfect mother is so caring and supportive of all the family that it is assumed that she will take on anyone who needs her, whenever they need her.

Dorothy was available now that her girls had left home and so could take over looking after her parents. The doctor had inadvertently voiced this assumption to her. Her sister had been more blunt: "You haven't anything else to stop you looking after them. I'm working. I can't take time off work to help. You have all day – surely you can fit them in? How can you be so selfish? My own children are still at home, I hardly see my husband and my boss is just looking for an excuse not to promote me."

Whenever Dorothy mentioned these comments, she would say: "I know they're right. I should be able to cope. I don't know why I find it all so difficult."

What Dorothy wants for herself

I asked Dorothy what she wanted for herself. Her wishes were simple – to have time for her own friends and hobbies, more time with Henry and less time with her parents.

I asked her if anyone else had asked her what she wanted. The look on her face told me the answer. Dorothy was not used to being asked what she wanted. She had been invisible in her family for many years. She was the carer. It was only now, when she had become tearful and unhappy, that others had begun asking her questions or complaining about the change in her. As long as she looked after everyone else without complaining or being obviously unhappy, she was invisible as an individual.

Dorothy now took some significant first steps towards taking control of her own life. She talked with Henry about what it was she wanted both for herself and for the two of them. As a result, over the following weeks and months, she became stronger, finding herself able to enjoy life and forging a better relationship with her husband. Then she talked with her parents, explaining how she needed some time for herself. She also discussed this with her brothers and sisters, refusing to take on all the responsibility for their parents' day-to-day care. While this caused some tensions between them, any change was an improvement for Dorothy so she stuck to her guns. Over time, her relationship with her parents improved as her resentment at having to go see them lessened now that she was not required to go every day. There were down days, of course, but Dorothy kept what she wanted clear in her mind.

When things stay the same because the children will *not* leave

Increasingly there are mothers faced with a truly difficult dilemma: their children are living at home even when they are in their mid-20s or older. The perfect mother is faced with an unthinkable choice: continue to care for her adult children or do things for herself. The mother trying to maintain her status of perfect mother is in a predicament, never realizing that, by continuing to be invisible to her family, she is not encouraging her children to grow into adults themselves (*see* Chapter 11).

What is happening in these families? Certainly the perfect mothers continue in their roles of invisible, self-sacrificing carers. Take the story of Miriam Pollock, reported in the *Sunday Telegraph* (London)[11]. She and her husband found themselves banished from their own home one cold evening because their

82

two sons, both lawyers in their 20s, were hosting a dinner party and felt that their parents' presence would cramp their style. When the Pollocks wanted to return home later in the evening, they had to creep in the back door and upstairs so as not to be heard. "It was as if they were the parents and we were the teenagers who had stayed out beyond curfew," said Miriam.

The Pollocks decided to act, and banished their sons to rented accommodation. The brothers were shocked at their parents' actions – and at the true cost of rent, electricity bills and so on. One of the sons said it all: "Why leave? Mum did the washing, Dad paid the bills."

The research organisation Mintel found that, in the UK, more than 55 per cent of young men aged 24 now live in their parents' home, while 35 per cent of young women remain there.[12]

One of the common difficulties with adult children remaining at home is a failure to renegotiate the rules. The perfect mother continues to do all the things she always did for her children when they were younger: the washing, the cleaning, the cooking of meals and the toleration of selfish, thoughtless behaviour. Even when the children have left home once, to go to college, and then returned, it is all too easy for the perfect mother to slip back into her previous role of "do it all".

Common themes

All of the perfect mothers in this chapter have things in common. They all tried to achieve the ideal of motherhood, which encompasses more than looking after the children. The perfect mother cares for her partner, her children, her extended family (including her partner's relatives) and anyone else who asks for help. The perfect mother never says "no"; she merely tries to figure out how everyone and everything can be juggled to fit. Saying "no" is the behaviour of a bad mother, one who is selfish and does not take into account other people's needs. After all, the perfect mother does not put her work or her needs first. Her life is focused on caring and this is her greatest weakness. It is an impossible task striving always to be the perfect mother. Eventually everything comes tumbling down.

One of the only means of communicating for these invisible perfect mothers is to become helpless in some way. In their tearful sadness, they are saying: "Look at me. This is all too much. I can't do this any more. I have needs, too. I want you to see me. I'm not invisible."

PART TWO

Making yourself visible: adult mothers

9

Perfect mothers, invisible women, lots of Prozac

The cost of being invisible

When women become invisible to others in their roles as mothers, they tend to lose themselves. Perfect mothers become selfless in their attempts to please everyone and so lose sight of what they want. They often feel overwhelmed by the pressures on them. It is not hard to understand why when you examine the position of the invisible woman in the diagram below.

What is the result of becoming this non-person, this self-less person? It is foolish to believe that people have no preferences of their own or nothing they want just for themselves. We all have these needs – it is part of the human condition. Without wants and needs, we are nothing, and we communicate this to others.

A perfect mother who never thinks of herself buries her own feelings. The sorrow, resentment and anger grow within, creating conflict that may lead to illness, anxiety and depression.

Mother's little helper: Valium

In the 1960s, the tranquillizers Valium (generic name: diazepam) became known as "mother's little helper". Women in their

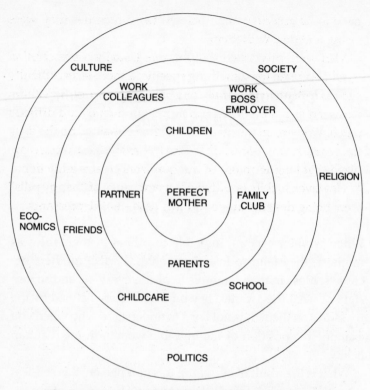

The pressures and influences on the *invisible woman*

millions were prescribed the drug to ease their anxiety, their depression and their sadness. If a woman went to her doctor saying she couldn't cope with everything at home or if she cried about her relationship with her husband, the doctor, feeling he had to help, would prescribe Valium. It did not change anything at home, of course, but it meant that the woman was sedated enough not to feel her sadness or anger so could cope with all the demands on her. It was hailed as the "happy pill", something that everyone could take to feel better. Because of this drug, it seemed, no one had to change. Women did not have to be assertive and confront the difficulties they were facing and deal with them.

Men were prescribed Valium, too. Usually a prescription would be given for something specific, a short-term difficulty such as a death in the family or a big event at work. So Valium was seen as a temporary crutch to help men over a difficult patch. Women, on the other hand, often remained on the drug for years. It was not until the early 1980s that it was recognized that long-term use of tranquillizers creates addiction.

However, luckily or unluckily, a new range of "happy pills" were being developed around this time – antidepressants.

Mother's new little helpers: Prozac and friends

By the 1990s, antidepressants had been refined into much safer and more effective drugs than Valium and the other tranquillizers. Antidepressants such as Prozac (generic name: fluoxetine) have their clinical usefulness and, when used appropriately, are very helpful for people suffering from clinical depression. But clinical depression is quite different from what is commonly understood as "depression".

Clinical depression may be so incapacitating that the person stops eating, sleeping, dressing or even washing him/herself. Obviously this incapacity needs treating, both medically with antidepressants and psychologically with therapy.

However, what most of us call "depression" is actually sadness, stress or difficulty in coping with our daily lives. But should we take pills to help make us happy with something that makes us sad? Should we take a happy pill to cope with a situation that is too difficult for us to handle? Surely a more logical and constructive approach would be to tackle the problems that have caused us the stress or the sadness.

Since 1995 in the UK, the prescribing of Prozac-like medication has increased by 700 per cent.[13] It is interesting to note how, compared with men, British women are treated differently by their doctors: Prozac and its counterparts are prescribed to approximately 1 in 12 women but only to 1 in 26 men.[14]

Read the following sections to try to sort out whether you are clinically depressed and therefore need to seek a doctor's help, or whether you are suffering from a milder form of depression, anxiety or stress that might respond to steps you can take yourself.

Symptoms of clinical depression: a checklist

The checklist below includes thoughts and feelings all of us experience sometime. However, if they last for more than a few weeks and would not be considered the natural response to a loss or upset such as the death of a loved one, you should seek medical help.

1   Is your mood low and depressed for most of the day, especially when you wake and get up in the morning?
2   Have you felt much less interest or pleasure in activities that you previously enjoyed?
3   Have you had a significant change in weight, either an increase or a decrease?
4   Have you had a change in appetite, either an increase or a decrease?
5   Has your sleep pattern altered? Are you unable to stay awake or unable to sleep, or has there been a change in when you wake up or go to sleep?
6   Do you feel really tired every day?
7   Do you feel worthless or a burden to others most days?

8 Most days, do you feel unable to concentrate or make decisions?
9 Have you had repeated thoughts about death in general, your own death or even how to commit suicide?
10 Have you had these feelings and thoughts for more than a few weeks?

If you have answered "yes" to more than three of these questions, there is cause for concern and you should not allow things to drift much longer before going to see your doctor. **If you have answered 'yes' to question 9, you should seek help immediately from your doctor or local mental health department.**

In the meantime, you may want to consider whether there are things about your life, either now or in your past, that may be contributing to your feelings of sadness and helplessness. Look at the questions later in this chapter on what you should consider before medication.

Your doctor may be able to put you in touch with a counsellor or psychologist to talk through the possible causes of your sadness and also to look at how you can make changes to help you feel better. This may be done with or without medication. Many women try counselling first, before starting any medication, and then discover they feel better.

For those women who have buried their own needs and become selfless mothers, depression is a common result. There are also feelings of loss – the loss of individual identity and purpose.

Symptoms of post-natal depression

Post-natal depression is a type of depression that comes on within four weeks of the birth of a baby. It is different from the "baby blues" that almost all mothers go through a few days after the birth. The questions above concerning depression apply equally for post-natal depression. But other feelings and thoughts may also occur, such as an excessive fear of germs, objects or situations that might harm your baby.

If you experience any of these, it is worth talking about them to someone you trust. Your doctor or health visitor can also help you. Many new mothers fear that their baby will be "taken away" if they speak openly about their fear of not being able to cope. This is not true, except in the very extreme and rare cases when the mother is no longer aware of what she is doing.

It is interesting to note that, despite the usually accepted notion that post-natal depression is rooted in the hormonal changes that occur after childbirth, many adoptive mothers also experience something parallel to post-natal depression. This suggests that the feelings of confusion, shock, insecurity and inadequacy, the fear of being unable to look after the baby, the woman's feelings of disappointment over the baby or even in her role as a mother – all of which are found in post-natal depression – arise from something other than hormonal changes.[15]

Following a difficult delivery, such as a forceps or Caesarean delivery, the new mother may also feel guilt. She often believes that she has failed as a woman and mother since she was unable to complete what is generally seen as a "natural" female biological task. This feeling of failure can join with guilt at not being a perfect mother and may result in depression. Exploring the source of these feelings and the unrealistic expectations many women have concerning a "natural delivery" may be more effective at relieving the depression than a prescription for Prozac.

Post-traumatic stress disorder (PTSD): a checklist

Giving birth has always been regarded as a "natural" process and so the effects on the mother of what may be quite a traumatic experience have been overlooked or, worse, disregarded. Recently, however, there has been a growing recognition that some new mothers are actually traumatized by the births of their babies.

If the birth did not go as planned, this may be enough to produce the symptoms and feelings that would normally be associated with a more "traumatic" event such as a road accident. Some women report undergoing painful and frightening experiences as a part of the management of their labour, such as feeling out of control, having all decisions made by others, being strapped down before the administration of anaesthesia, a painful invasion of the body by forceps or other medical procedures. This combination of pain, fear and loss of control may lead to the typical symptoms of PTSD because of a traumatic birth experience.

Read through the following questions to see if you are experiencing any of the symptoms of PTSD:

1   Do images, thoughts or feelings of the birth keep returning to your mind?
2   Do these images, thoughts or feelings of the birth keep intruding into your thoughts unbidden?
3   Have you continued to have distressing dreams about the birth?
4   Do you find yourself acting or feeling as though you are going through or about to go through the birth again?
5   Do you become very distressed if you see, hear or smell something that reminds you of the birth?
6   Do you avoid anything that will remind you of the birth?

7   Do you find that you cannot recall large periods of time
    around the birth itself?

8   Since the birth, have you noticed that you can't concen-
    trate as well as before, that you become angry more easily,
    that you have a tendency to be easily startled or that you
    don't sleep as well as you used to?

If you have answered "yes" to more than three of these questions, you might benefit from some therapy, which would include talking about the birth with someone sympathetic to
the idea of birth being a traumatic process. Let your doctor
know that you are having problems and make it clear that
you feel that you need some support.

Symptoms of anxiety: a checklist

Remember that everyone suffers from anxiety at times – anyone who doesn't isn't human! However, constant anxiety –
which is very unpleasant – should be a cause for concern. The
following checklist is concerned with feelings and thoughts
that have lasted for more than a few weeks.

1   Are you usually anxious and worried about something?

2   Most days, do you tremble or twitch or do you feel shaky?

3   Do you frequently feel aches, pain and soreness because
    you are so tense?

4   Most days, do you feel short of breath or as if you are
    being smothered?

5   Do you often notice that your heart is racing?

6   Do you have difficulty swallowing or feel a 'lump in your
    throat' most days?

7   Do you frequently have difficulty concentrating or notice
    that your "mind goes blank"?

8   Do you have trouble falling or staying asleep most nights?

9 Are you more irritable than you would like to be with those close to you a lot of the time?

If you answer "yes" to more than three of the questions, consider seeking help or taking steps to help yourself. Anxiety and feelings of panic are common in someone who is already highly stressed. Rather than treating the anxiety with tablets, have you considered reducing the sources of your stress? What makes your life difficult? Would becoming a more visible adult mother help you?

Pre-menstrual syndrome

Pre-menstrual syndrome (PMS) is a term used to define a cluster of symptoms – that is, a "syndrome" – that occur in the week or so before the menstrual period. It was first known as "pre-menstrual tension", but this term was disgarded when it was realized that the symptoms included more than irritability and tension. There is still heated debate about whether this is a physical disorder caused by alternations in hormone levels or a psychological one. The most common symptoms are nervous tension, mood swings, irritability, anxiety, fatigue and headaches. Physical changes can include bloatedness, weight gain and even cravings for sweets and other refined carbohydrates.

Women often report that they fall out with their partners at this time in their menstrual cycle. During years of seeing women for psychological therapy, it has often been apparent to me that many experience a loss of control, shout angry complaints and/or voice their frustrations during this pre-menstrual phase. However, could this be because these complaints and frustrations are never talked about, adult to adult, within the relationship? It seems to me that the pre-menstrual women are simply giving expression to the tensions that are present throughout their daily lives; it's just that, at this time, they are simply unable to contain their resentment any longer.

Rather than dismissing these "rantings of hormonal women", perhaps their partners should actually be taking more notice. It is at this time that even the most timid, least assertive women have an excuse to voice their complaints and wishes for themselves. Some therapists have even labelled PMS as "Pre-Menstrual Sanity"![16] The woman's valid complaints are being expressed at this pre-menstrual time because her normally high level of self-control is lessened.

The menopause

Many women dread this time of life, although they are often unsure why it is thought of so badly. Often the stories and beliefs about the menopause arise from within our families and we carry them with us as family truths and absolute truths.

Just like pre-menstrual syndrome, the menopause is experienced as a cluster of symptoms, although it can be positively diagnosed by a blood test to determine whether there has been a drop in the levels of hormones usually required to maintain menstruation. While some women sail through the menopause with hardly any symptoms, others find that they experience everything from mood swings to hot flushes. Everyone is different.

However, once women reach a "certain age", usually but not always their 40s and 50s, they are told that their frustrations and tears are due to the beginnings of "the change", no matter what the true cause is. As I have already said in the section on pre-menstrual syndrome (*above*), it is all too easy to dismiss real distress by blaming "hormones". However, it is equally foolish to ignore symptoms if hormonal changes are taking place.

Before you consider medication . . .
. . . Consider the following questions:

1 How long have you felt this way?
2 Did something happen a month or two before you started feeling this way and which was upsetting or difficult for you?
3 Do you feel that you have no time for yourself?
4 Do other people leave you feeling criticized or bad about yourself?
5 Do you wonder who you are?
6 Do you feel that you have lost yourself?
7 Do you feel invisible to others who should care about you?
8 Do you resent your partner for not helping you with the children enough?
9 Do you feel that no one understands how hard it is for you?
10 Do you feel more depressed or anxious when at home?
11 Do you wish someone else would care for your children?
12 Do you daydream about returning to work?
13 Do you daydream about giving up work so that you could leave behind the conflict of being both a mother and and an employee?
14 Do you wish that you could be more assertive?
15 Do you feel unable to go against other people's expectations that you will look after them or do things for them?
16 Do you wish that you could be a better mother?
17 Do you think that you would benefit by becoming a visible adult mother?

If you have answered "yes" to any of these questions, there are steps that you can take.

Steps towards feeling better about yourself – and becoming an adult mother in the process!

Study carefully the following parts of this book, which may prove particularly helpful:

- *Chapter 15: Talking together* – share how you feel with your partner.
- *Chapter 3: The influence of our family on our style of motherhood* – expect to be visible and treated with respect by the family club.
- *Chapter 10: What stops you from being who you want to be?* – decide for yourself by examining absolute truths.
- *Chapter 14: Saying what you want: assertiveness* – learn how to express your needs and desires.
- *Chapter 11: Adult mothers, visible women – what does it mean?* – your adult approach to your children.
- *Chapter 12: The adult mothers' charter* – stop feeling guilty!

If you feel you need more serious help: visiting your doctor

If you decide that you feel bad enough to seek medical help, possibly including medication, you should still seek the reasons for your depression or anxiety. No one develops these problems without a reason.

As well as considering medication, talk to your doctor about seeing someone to whom you can talk, such as a counsellor working in the practice or a referral to a psychologist. It is not good enough any more for a woman, especially a mother, to be prescribed a drug merely to stop her from being anxious or sad. The prescription puts nothing right and may simply encourage her to cope with an intolerable situation at home or in another part of her life. In addition, if a mother is unhappy and is told that the answer to her problem lies in pills, what sort of message does that give to her children?

If your partner supports your need for help, take him with you. It is still a sad fact that, if a woman goes to see a doctor and says that she is feeling anxious or depressed, she is not generally taken seriously. A woman whose partner accompanies her and says: "Help her" tends to receive more attention and more offers of help.

10

What stops you from being who you want to be?

Have you ever wanted to do something and found yourself unable or unwilling to do it? Of course, you have, because it happens to all of us. But have you found yourself wanting to do something that other people do and still stopped yourself from doing it? For instance, do you long to have a day off – to go window shopping or spend the day reading or simply sleeping? What is stopping you?

It is all too easy to ask these questions and not understand how difficult it is to change our lives. Change is uncomfortable and this stops us from moving towards something that we would like to do. The three most commonly voiced reasons for not doing something are:

- *Myself*: how I think I ought to behave, who I think I am.
- *Other people*: their criticism of me, their pressure on me to behave a certain way.
- *Money!*

In reality, there are only two reasons, because the pressure and criticism of other people only affect you if you allow them to.

When you feel sad, you could run off, leave your family and go stay with friends far away. You don't. Why not? At times, you may dream of doing something outrageous, but you stop yourself doing it. Why? Because you make choices in your life even if they are not obvious. You choose to look after your children, or you choose to put yourself last sometimes (or often). Sometimes your choice will be in your best interest. You may make it because you feel others will disapprove of the alternative – this choice may or may not be in your best interest. You are free to choose, but you may not feel strong enough to do so because of the consequences.

When you tell yourself that you must do something or must *not* do something, where does this belief come from? As discussed earlier, most of our beliefs about ourselves and how we should be come from our families and our culture.

As an adult, it may be time for you to re-examine these beliefs or *absolute truths.*

Fill in the following diagram to work out the layers of responsibility and pressure on you.

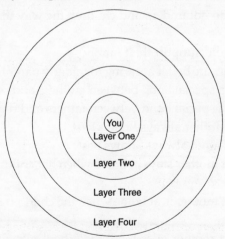

Diagram 2   What influences you.

Layer One : Who or What influences your choices *most.*
Layer Two : Who or What influences your choices *next.*
Layer Three : and so on.
Refer to Diagram 1 as a guide to help you.

What stops you from being who you want to be?

Some absolute truths – which ones apply to you?

Read through the following list of absolute truths:

- A normal woman will want children of her own.
- A woman cannot expect to keep a man if she refuses him a child.
- The woman who is infertile has failed in her duty to reproduce.
- The fertile woman who chooses not to have a child is selfish.
- A woman's most fulfilling moment is when her newborn baby looks into her eyes.
- A woman does not really feel love until she has a baby of her own.
- A woman shows her most unselfish love when raising a child.
- A perfect mother always puts her children first.
- Men cannot look after children as well as women.
- Fathers do not understand children the way their mothers do.
- Men should support their family.
- Daughters are better at caring for elderly parents than sons.
- There is a special bond between mothers and sons.
- There is a special bond between fathers and daughters.
- (Grand)Mother always knows best.
- (Grand)Father always knows best.
- A perfect mother stays at home when her children are very young.
- A perfect mother is at home when the children return from school.
- A perfect mother goes to all the school plays and assemblies.
- A perfect mother does not allow her job to interfere with being a mother.

- A perfect mother does not leave her children to go out and have fun.
- A perfect father is responsible for his family's financial security.
- A perfect father should leave the cuddles and kisses to the mother.
- A perfect father measures his success by the achievements of his children.

Of these absolute truths, which ones have you heard spoken by members of your family club? Which ones have you always believed? Which ones do you think are making you feel a failure? Which ones are stopping you from doing what you (and your partner) want to do? Which ones do you question now?

If you recognize any of these absolute truths as beliefs that you or your family club hold, ask yourself:

- Does this have to be true?
- Why?
- What do I think?

Some family truths – which ones apply to you?

Read through the following list of family truths:

- Mothers in our family never work full-time.
- Mothers in our family do not let their children misbehave like other children.
- Our family always celebrates birthdays together.
- Our family always gets together at Christmas.
- Our family looks after each other.
- Our family is closer than others around us.
- No one in our family has ever got divorced.

- No one in our family misbehaves.
- Mothers in our family have their priorities right.
- Fathers in our family work hard to support their partners and children.
- The oldest son takes responsibility for dealing with his brothers and sisters.
- The oldest daughter takes responsibility for caring for others in her family.

Of these family truths, which ones have you heard spoken by members of your family club? Which ones have you always believed? Which ones do you think are making you feel a failure? Which ones are stopping you from doing what you (and your partner) want to do? Which ones do you question now?

If you recognize any of these family truths as beliefs that you or your family club hold, ask yourself:

- Does this have to be true?
- Why?
- What do I think?

Creating a family diagram

Or, looking for what makes you the same as your mother!

Looking at your family club members and gaining an insight into how the club works will help you discover the pressures under which you operate. This will, in turn, help you to decide for yourself how you want to be.

It helps to express the workings of the family club in graphic form. To do this, you will need several large sheets of paper, preferably from an artist's pad. The more members you have in your extended family, the more paper you will need. Leave a space around each person's name so that you can add key words such as "gentle", "angry", "dominating", "passive".

Sit down and draw up a family tree for your immediate family.

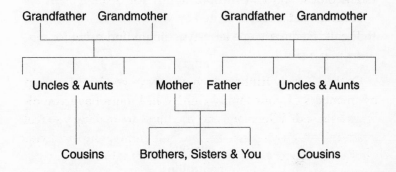

Your diagram may be fairly simple like the one above or quite complex if there have been a number of divorces, deaths, remarriages, etc.

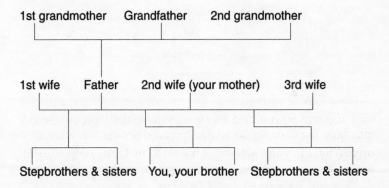

Next to each name write a summary of what that individual was/is like, including career achievements and anything else important. Look at the various partnerships in the family. Who was dominant in each partnership? Did one person in each couple always bow to the wishes of the other? Look particularly at how work and children were managed within your family.

Next to each person, write key words summarizing your thoughts. Here are some terms you might find useful:

angry

sad

happy

loving

anxious

controlling

passive

difficult

independent

successful

sulky

fun

generous

temperamental

Now look at your parents and grandparents, and the uncles and aunts to whom you are close. Whose disapproval strikes fear into other members of the family?

Key questions to ask:

- Who did what in each partnership?
- Who was dominant in each couple?
- Who is close to whom? On your diagram, draw a double line linking people who are very close and zig-zag lines

between those who are always in conflict with each other.

- Are there similarities between family members?
- Who looked after the children?
- What style of parenting did they use – harsh, soft, violent, praising?
- Who was helpful to the children – and why?
- Who was not involved with the children – and why?
- What attitudes towards children did they display?
- What influence do they have on you now?
- Do you fear their disapproval?
- Do you seek their approval?

A completed family diagram will probably look something like the one on page 108 (Diagram 3). As new ideas come to you, you can add to your diagram.

The next thing to do is to ask your partner to express his thoughts about your family. Don't be surprised if he says things about members of your family that make you feel uncomfortable or with which you disagree. Allow your partner to voice his opinions so you can hear an outsider's view of your club members. Remember, if your partner says your mother doesn't listen to anyone or your father never has a point of view about his children, this could be a valuable insight for you. You are the one inside the family club and you can't always see its members as others see them. Write down your partner's key points on your family diagram.

Once you have completed a diagram for your own family, do one for your partner's family. When you have completed both, place them side by side and look at the similarities as well as the differences. You may be surprised at how similar they are, but this may be a reason why you were both attracted to each other – similar backgrounds and emotional upbringings can bring people together.

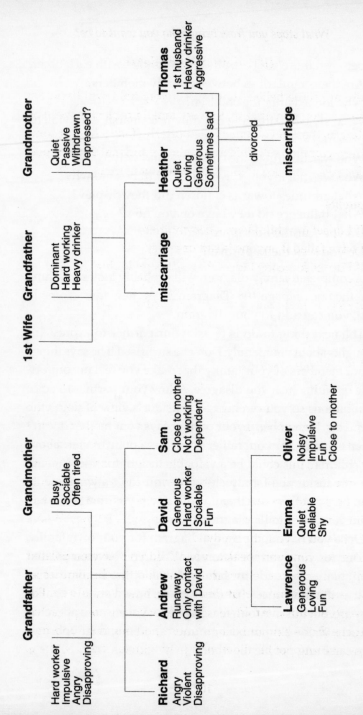

Diagram 3   A complete family diagram

Self-defeating beliefs

There are some beliefs that can actively hold you back. For instance, you may find that a very small problem leaves you feeling as though you have failed utterly. Take a look at some of these common self-defeating beliefs – and matching impossible tasks – and see if you recognize any of them.

Thoughts

- If I upset my child, I am a bad mother.
- I have failed if anyone is sad or angry.
- If I upset someone I love, they will stop loving me.
- If I say what I really think, no one will like me.
- If I say what I really want, no one will like me.

Impossible task

- I must keep everyone happy (or I have failed as a mother and wife).

When they say "no" or speak sharply to their children who then become upset, many mothers feel bad. As soon as the child cries or looks upset, the guilt starts or the belief that to have made your child cry means that you are a bad mother. The consequence of this self-defeating belief is that the only way for you to feel that you are a perfect mother or just to feel good yourself is to keep your child happy at all times. Where does this leave you, the mother?

The next time you speak to your children or to your partner or other members of your family club and they become upset as a result, remember that this may be how it should be. For example, if you have told your child that you are disappointed that she did not do the chores you asked her to do and as a result she will not be allowed to play with her friends, she is likely to become upset or withdrawn. If you are someone who always tries to keep people happy, you will feel uncomfortable at this reaction and so will probably let your daughter out to play with her friends to make her happy again. However, the lesson you have taught your daughter is that you do not have to be listened to at any time and that tears will allow her to get her own way. You are left feeling defeated even though your daughter is happier. You should instead realize that it is perfectly acceptable to say "no", to disappoint your daughter if she has disappointed you by not doing her chores. You are being an adult mother teaching your daughter a valuable lesson for her future life – for instance, about meeting deadlines.

For a further discussion along these lines, look at Chapter 23: *Visible adult mothers, successful children*.

Thoughts

- I want everyone to approve of my choices.
- I want everyone to understand me (and so approve).

Impossible task

- I must please everyone.

This simply will never happen. There is always bound to be someone who disapproves of what you do. Striving to make everyone approve of or like you is an impossible task and will take all your time and energy. The only person whose approval you need in order to choose what to do with your life is . . . *you*.

Thoughts

- Only I am responsible for how my child behaves.
- If my child misbehaves, it must be my fault – I am a bad mother.

- If my child upsets someone else, I must apologize on her behalf.
- If my child fails, I must try harder – his failure is my failure.

Impossible task

- I must be aware of everything my children are doing and ensure that they are good at all times.

The energy it takes perfect mothers to try to achieve this impossible task is enormous. Perfect mothers feel themselves to be failures every time their children misbehave. As the children grow older and start acting independently, perfect mothers – so concerned about preventing failure and mistakes – will discourage true independence.

However, adult mothers recognize the impossibility of being constantly responsible for preventing their children's bad behaviour and mistakes. Instead adult mothers are able to separate themselves from their children and have them take some responsibility for themselves. This allows the growing children to learn from their mistakes and to judge how certain behaviours affect others in the real world, beyond the family club.

Thoughts

- I need to put others first.
- I cannot put myself first.
- I must not say "no".
- I must be happy all the time.
- I must not be angry.
- If I am upset, I must not let anyone see.

Impossible task

- I must put anyone and everyone before myself.

The woman who tries to put everyone first is bound to collapse from exhaustion or erupt into uncontrollable rage! Putting one's own needs aside whenever there is another person present merely leads to the build-up of resentment and feelings of not being seen. This perfect mother becomes a seething, resentful invisible woman.

Thoughts

- If we have a problem in the family, we must keep it secret – or others will see that I am a bad mother.
- If we have a problem with our relationship, we must struggle on. If we don't, I will have failed to make the relationship work.

Impossible task

- If we have a problem, I personally must find a way to solve it without help.

This is the trap of family secrets. Everything has to be kept within the family club; the outside world must never know what is happening. This policy seems to work until there is a true crisis and the façade collapses. Talking together with your partner or family may help during such a crisis, but seeking help from a therapist may be essential if you are going to tackle the root of the problem.

11

Adult mothers, visible women – what does it mean?

Taking responsibility for your own life

Becoming adult mothers means taking responsibility for ourselves. Of course, we all believe that we are already adults, that we make clear decisions for ourselves and our families and that we shoulder our share of responsibilities. But do we really? Earlier in this book, you encountered two women who tried their hardest to be the mothers that they thought they wanted to be. Anne and Julie tried to be perfect mothers, but found that being so selfless made them invisible. They took on more than their share of responsibilities, but found that a lot of these responsibilities belonged to other people rather than to themselves.

Over the years, being a perfect mother has changed from trying to keep your children alive to giving your life to your children. In the 20th century, the acceptance of the psychoanalytic approach to development meant that responsibility for a child's healthy emotional development has been at the expense of the mother – she constantly worries whether the last harsh word or the latest indulgence will actually result in her child developing into a disturbed, emotionally dependent adult. Therapists have minutely examined the bond between mother and child. Family therapists – who focus beyond the individual and examine the family as a whole – still describe the over-involved mother and the emotionally distant father.

Although there are exceptions, traditional expectations of women – and of mothers, in particular – pervade all professions and walks of life. And it is hardly surprising that they do. Each and every theorist, each and every politician, journalist or psychologist comes from a family where it is likely that the mother strove towards the unattainable role of perfect mother, yet her efforts often went completely unrecognized and unrewarded.

However, with the advent of the idea of the "good enough" mother, devised by the child psychiatrist and psychoanalyst Donald Winnicott (1896–1971)[17], there was finally recognition that a mother could not be and should not strive to be perfect or selfless. However, having "good enough" as a goal may seem distinctly inadequate to some mothers. If a child who has worked hard on homework proudly holds up the work at school only to be told by the teacher that it is just "good enough", wouldn't he or she be disappointed? All those hours of work and imagination poured into the homework dismissed as "good enough" rather than good – or great or perfect? We all want to be better mothers. Can we be better mothers by accepting ourselves not as perfect but as adult mothers doing our best?

Becoming an adult mother

What is the true purpose of motherhood today? We take the decision to bring a new life into the world with the hope and expectation that all will be wonderful. What do we want for this child? What do we want for ourselves? We want to raise a child and teenager who is happy, who grows into a young

114

adult who can do well in the world. We would like our son or daughter to be able to get along well with others. We want to bring up a person who can look after him/herself and go successfully out into the world.

Women put all the time and energy they can into being perfect mothers, but what do perfect mothers do? They strive to take care of their children's every need while becoming invisible women themselves. But do these selfless perfect mothers, striving to do the best they can for their children, help the children to grow into the kind of adults they want them to be?

Thinking about motherhood in this way leads us to think about ourselves. What are we communicating to our children when we sacrifice ourselves for them – our individuality and even our visibility within the family? Are we telling our daughters that this is what is expected of them? Are we telling our sons that it is their future partner's role not to be a soul mate or equal but to become self-sacrificing and invisible, just like his mother? Is this what sons want when they meet the carefree, exuberant, fun-filled girlfriend of their dreams? Do they want her to disappear under the heavy burden of family club membership and absolute truths?

Should we not instead be communicating that we as mothers are human beings, adults who share parenting with our children's fathers? Should we not be teaching our children that we all have needs, we all have dreams and we all have to have time for ourselves? Should we not be teaching our children that they are not the centre of anyone's life, but part of a web of ever-growing, ever-changing relationships where needs and wishes are respected?

Recognizing your worth as an individual

How many times a day do you put someone else first? Whether

it is a newborn baby, a teenager, your partner, a member of your family club or a friend, how often do your own plans go out of the window?

One of the most difficult changes for many mothers to make is to accept that they do have a right to their own feelings and needs. Before the birth of their first child, most women accept this and expect other people to recognize this fact. However, the whole concept of perfect motherhood ignores the needs of the individual woman who has become a mother. Her over-whelming tiredness and the anger and resentment she feels towards others, including her own children, are ignored at best or condemned at worst.

Honesty is needed to ensure a more balanced and success-ful motherhood. Both this and a growing self-confidence will come from regarding yourself as an adult – an adult mother. After all, you are an adult in other walks of life. You are treated as an adult at work; you make decisions and accept responsi-bility for them. If you make a mistake, you accept the conse-quences and then go on. This is what adults do. This is how adults behave. Adults say clearly what they want, know why they want it and take responsibility. Adults also expect to be treated a certain way – with dignity and respect. Do you remem-ber longing to be an adult when you were a teenager? Most of us yearned for adulthood at that age so we could do what we wanted and have fun without a parent or teacher telling us "no". As an adult mother, it is important to remember that you are also responsible for ensuring that you have fun!

How does becoming an adult mother make you a better mother?

Becoming a confident and assertive mother helps you to become a better mother. At first, this may not seem obvious, but your children will see how you conduct yourself and will learn from you. If you are always put last by others, they will come to believe that this is an acceptable way of being. If they are able to manipulate you, then ultimately they will accept this position for themselves or will treat others the same way.

A constant fear of failing as a mother means that many women do everything for their children. The result, of course, is that these children are unable to do anything for themselves. They become dependent on their mothers who, in turn, spend all their time caring for their children. The more time they spend caring for their children, the more of a perfect mother they feel - while actually failing to prepare their children for the real world of school and, later, adulthood.

Being confident will enable you to encourage new skills and abilities in your children. Teaching them the skills they need to cope at school, to look after themselves, to interact with other people, to stand up to bullies and to take a pride in their own abilities requires you to have your own self-confidence. Have you noticed how children who are bullied at school are often the offspring of very nice parents who never want to offend anyone? I'm not suggesting that, as a parent, you should stop being nice to others, simply that others should not *always* come first.

Preventing that all-too-common feeling of being over-whelmed and overloaded with responsibilities for others will enable you to stand back and look at your children as individuals for perhaps the first time. Do you know what your children want for themselves? Do you really know what they are capable of or do you always do everything for them? How constrained are your children by the expectations of others – particularly the family club?

The adult mother is able to say "no" and not feel guilty. Always saying "yes" gives a false impression of what the world will be like.

Becoming an adult mother means that you will communicate your own needs and be open to hear the needs of others. Instead of feeling invisible and powerless under the pressure of other people's expectations, the adult mother takes her place alongside everyone and everything else.

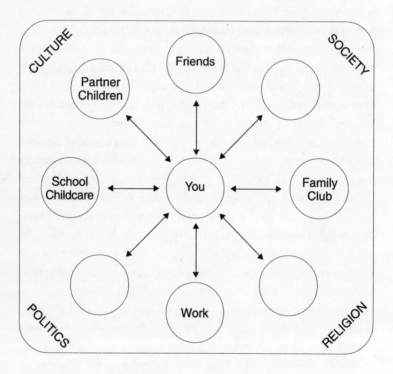

Diagram 4   Pressures and influences on an *adult mother*

12

The adult mother's charter

Your rights as an adult mother: becoming visible

Your individual rights as an adult mother

- I have the right to take care of myself.
- I have the right to my own personal space and time.
- I have the right to determine and honour my own priorities.
- I have the right to have my needs and wants respected by others, including my children.

Your freedom to choose

- I have the right to make my own decisions.
- I have the right to make choices in everything I do, for myself, for my children and for others.
- I have the right to make my own decisions based on my feelings and my judgment.
- I have the right to change my mind at any time.

Your rights to be a human being

- I have the right to make mistakes and not have to be perfect.
- I have the right to be uniquely me without feeling I'm not good enough.
- I have the right to be angry at someone I love.
- I have the right to feel scared and to say I'm afraid.

- I have the right to experience and then let go of guilt, fear and shame.
- I have the right to be happy.
- I have the right to make friends and feel comfortable around people.
- I have the right to be playful, relaxed and frivolous if I choose to be.
- I have the right to be flexible and to be comfortable with this.
- I have the right to give and receive unconditional love.
- I have the right to change and grow.

Your rights to be treated as an adult mother

- I have the right to dignity and respect from all.
- I have the right to all of my feelings, not just those that other people want me to feel.
- I have the right to bring to an end conversations with people who make me feel put down, humiliated, dismissed or uncomfortable.

Your rights to expect things from others

- I have the right *not* to be responsible for others' behaviour, actions, feelings or problems, including those of my children.
- I have the right to expect honesty from others.
- I have the right to communicate with others so I may be understood.

Your responsibilities as an adult mother

Your responsibilities to yourself

- To take responsibility for your own life.

The adult mother's charter

- To recognize who owns the problem.
- To stop blaming others for your life.
- To stop waiting for others to change.
- To look at how *you* can change things.
- To recognize yourself as an individual with needs of your own.
- To recognize others as individuals with needs of their own.
- To believe that no one has an automatic right to come before you.
- To say what you want when you want to.
- To be prepared for others to try to change you back.
- To be able to distance yourself from other people's conflicts.
- To trust your own feelings. If you feel angry, ask yourself why. If you feel good, ask yourself why. If you feel that things are hopeless, ask yourself why.
- To be proud of your decisions. No one else has the right to question them – after all, only you know how you feel and why you made any particular choice.

Your responsibilities to your children

- To be truthful about your needs and feelings.
- To communicate as best you can.
- To act as an adult, showing adult behaviour.
- To take responsibility for adult decisions, those the children should not yet make.
- To take responsibility for mistakes and bad behaviour and then forget them.
- To encourage your children to accept their mistakes and then forget them.
- To make sure that you do *not* take out your frustrations on your children.

- To allow your children to be who they are.
- To teach your children responsibility.
- To encourage your children to see that they have choices.
- To encourage your children to say how they feel without fear.
- To teach your children how to care for themselves.
- To teach your children respect for their own feelings.
- To teach your children respect for other people's feelings.
- To be truthful with your children about family, relationships, death, etc.

Your responsibilities to your partner

- To be truthful about how you feel.
- To be truthful about what you want.
- To communicate as best you can.
- To listen to your partner's needs.
- To respect your partner's feelings even if you don't understand them.
- To offer a partnership in which you work together, *not* against each other.
- To put your partner above your parents or other members of the family club.
- To recognize that your priority is your immediate family, not your or his family club.

Your responsibilities to your family club

- To be truthful about how you feel.
- To be truthful about what you want.
- To communicate as best you can.
- To remember that your own family comes before the other members of the family club.

The adult mother's charter

- To remember that your needs are more important than those of the family club.

Remember: if everything stays the same, nothing good ever comes along.

13

Start looking at what you want to change

Stop blaming others for your life.
Stop waiting for other people to change.
Remember, if everything stays the same, nothing good
ever comes along.
It is natural to feel anxious or afraid when you are trying to
change things. This will pass.

Change is difficult. One of the main emotions we feel when considering change is anxiety. We are anxious about what will happen, how others will react and how we will cope with something new. All of these feelings are natural and happen to us all.

As adults, we should not expect life always to be smooth and easy. We often have to do things that we would not choose to do, such as cleaning toilets or paying bills, speaking up for ourselves to the boss or making a speech to a room full of strangers. But we do these things because we have to and because we know that, once done, we will have the satisfaction of knowing that we have achieved something despite our previous anxiety and fear.

Mothers all know the anxiety that comes when a woman discovers she is pregnant. Do you remember wondering, months before your baby was born, what the labour would be like? If you have had more than one child, you might remember the anxiety of knowing what labour was like "last time". This fear and anxiety are very real, but every woman knows that labour is the "natural" conclusion to her pregnancy and each one finds her own way to face it. Afterwards, having her baby in her arms becomes the explanation and justification for the pain. This is the same as facing personal change. We know it must come when we feel overwhelmed by the demands on us, but we also know that it might make us uncomfortable or anxious along the way.

Talking with someone you love about how you want to change can be nerve racking. Saying "no" for the first time to someone you love can make your heart pound, and the fear of terrible consequences can run round and round in your mind. Taking responsibility for your own decisions can make you nervous about making the "wrong" choice.

All of these feelings of fear, anxiety and worry are natural and part of being an adult. They are the cost of striving for what you want. However, each time you choose to change and ask for what you want, the anxiety decreases. You will learn that, even if you feel quite uncomfortable doing something for the first time, the feeling gradually becomes more manageable. This is the price of becoming visible to the rest of the world.

Ask yourself some key questions:

- What do I want?
- Can I see myself, in five years' time, still doing the same things as I am now?
- Am I the one responsible?

You and your health

- Do you take care of yourself physically?

- Do you take regular exercise?
- Do you take time to relax and do something frivolous, just for yourself?

Caring for yourself physically is important for everyone but particularly for mothers. Yet it is mothers at home with their children or balancing the demands of work and home life who do not make the time for themselves to exercise and relax. The results are obvious: mothers who are tired, physically run down and see no way of changing.

Physical fitness can be achieved in less than two hours a week and need not be complicated, expensive or involve lots of equipment. You should carry out some form of vigorous activity – such as walking, swimming, playing badminton or doing aerobics – for half an hour three times a week.

Consider your own exercise routine. The following suggestions may help:

- Walk or run regularly for 30 minutes three times per week.
- Buy some dumb-bell weights and teach yourself to use them.[18]
- Find out about local exercise classes. If you have young children, look for ones at sports centres with crèches or those that are open on weekends and in the evening. Try to find one where you can meet others in the same position as you.
- Sign up for an exercise class with a friend, to encourage both of you to keep attending.

Even a modest amount of regular exercise will leave you with more energy, help you sleep better and improve your overall health.

However, and especially at the start of your exercise programme, be careful and build up gradually to a regular routine. It is a good idea to consult your doctor before starting.

Time off for yourself

How often do you pamper yourself?

Indulging yourself – such as taking a long bath with fragrant oils – can make you feel special. It is important to recognize how important you are and to take time regularly to give yourself a treat. Using special bath oils or body cream can help you relax. It may also help you begin to like your body again after all the changes it underwent when you were pregnant and gave birth. Or you could let someone else pamper you by getting your partner or a friend to give you a massage or some other indulgence.

Spend some time thinking about what you enjoyed before you became a mother. Try to build time into your routine to enjoy these activities again – as well as any new ones you fancy – whether on your own, with friends or with your partner.

When did you last have a day off from being a mother so you could simply be yourself? You deserve it, just as you deserve time off from your place of employment. No one would expect an employee to work for 18 hours or more a day, seven days per week with no holidays. Why do we expect ourselves to do this in our role as mothers? Of course, we do not stop being mothers when we are away from our children – for instance, when they are at school or we are at work. However, it is important to have time for yourself so you do not become overwhelmed by your family or even disappear as an invisible woman.

Who or what stops you taking a day off?

- Is it you?
- Is it your partner?
- Is it the difficulty in finding someone else to care for the children?

There are many mothers who will not allow their children to be cared for away from home or be looked after by anyone other than themselves. They often feel that no one else can care for their children or understand them as well as they can. However, this closeness can become stifling if it continues over the years, both for the mother and for the children.

You and your own emotional needs

What do you need or want emotionally?

- Someone to listen to you?
- Someone who will give you a cuddle?
- To be closer to your partner?

Even as a mother, you still have emotional needs of your own. The moment of the birth of a first child changes everything. During your pregnancy, people may have fussed over you, making you feel special. Then, when the baby was born, you became the one who was expected to give – not receive.

Where does this leave mothers? Most struggle with this change but come to accept it. However, this self-sacrifice has a cost.

Your feelings will tell you what you need to change and what you want more of because it makes you happy. Women often dismiss their feelings as stupid or unimportant. However, your feelings *are* important and you should take notice of them. If you feel angry, ask yourself why. If you feel happy, ask yourself why. Your feelings will tell you what you need to know about your life and the people around you and what you need to change.

Keep a diary, one that lists your activities and interactions with other people. Make a note of how you feel after each activity or meeting. This will help give you clues about what upsets you and what or who makes you happy.

Activity	How did you feel?	Would you like to do it again?	What would you like to be different?
child's birthday party	very stressed	not really	more relaxed, less children, more help

Diagram 5   Diary of activities and meetings with others

You and your partner – time and interest

Ask yourself these questions:

- Before you had your children, what did you like to do with your partner?
- When did you last do this together?
- When did you last have fun together?

One of the difficulties of parenthood is the amount of time it takes. Even if you and your partner are both working together, talking together and agree on everything, it is hard to make time for each other without the children. But it is well worth the extra effort.

Think about your relationship and how much it will suffer if you don't devote some time to keeping it going. There are many mothers who have thrown their lives and energy into their children and then wake one morning to find that their partners have started relationships with younger single women! Often these affairs start because the "other woman" can spend a lot of time solely with the man, something he has missed at home. Less recognized are those mothers who also have affairs when their children are older because they too wake up one day and find that they have no relationship with their husbands other than one of practical domesticity. For such a woman, one of the great attractions of the "other man" is the interest he shows in her, in what she are doing and feeling.

Talk to your partner (*see* Chapter 15). Take time to tell him how you would like to be close, would like to share thoughts and dreams and feelings. Tell him that you would like to spend time relaxing with him out of the house, away from the children, but also at home, undisturbed, in the bath together, over a take-away – in fact, any time with the television turned off and the phone off the hook. The focus should be on each of you, not on problems or the chores you would like him to do!

You and your partner – time and interest and *sex*

For many couples, the arrival of children changes their sex lives. Why is this? The obvious reasons are tiredness when nursing small babies and the lack of privacy when the children are older. But often the real reason for the decline in sexual intimacy that you as a couple may once have enjoyed is a change in the expectations you have of yourselves. Once you see yourself as a mother, it may be difficult to be as carefree and sensual with your partner as you were before. An unrecognized belief in family truths may have led you or your partner to think that women who are mothers cannot also be sexual. This change in the way you see yourself or your partner may not be obvious until you examine how things are developing between you. (*See* Chapter 3 to remind yourself about family truths and absolute truths.)

Perfect mothers find it hard to give the sexual relationships with their partners a high priority in their lives. The needs and demands of children and family club members tend to come first. However, your needs as a woman do not go away once you are a mother. Your need for affection and support continues. Your need for shared sensual pleasure with your partner is as important as ever and, for many, becomes even more important.

If you feel unsupported and trapped in your role as mother, your desire for a sexual relationship is likely to diminish. If you feel that you shoulder too many responsibilities or are taken for granted by your partner, your desire for an intimate relationship is likely to be greatly reduced.

To have a healthy, intimate sexual relationship with your partner, you need to have a healthy, intimate emotional life. If

131

you are sharing the burdens of life and making time for each other to enjoy together some of its pleasures, the sexual part of the relationship is likely to flourish without attention. It is when the emotional sharing is poor that sexual relationships become difficult or non-existent. Talking to each other, saying clearly what you want, is the most helpful medicine for a flagging sexual relationship.

If you have lost the habit of being close and intimate with each other, start with some simple things that do not have to lead automatically to "sex". It is much more important to touch and be close simply for the warmth and sensual pleasure that it brings rather than have penetrative intercourse.

- Cuddle and touch each other affectionately during the day.
- Share a warm bath.
- Massage with body oils your "non-naughty bits" in a dimly lit room. It is not a disaster if you fall asleep – the main intention is for you to feel warm and relaxed!
- Massage each other with body oils in a dimly lit room, this time including the "naughty bits". Notice what he does and does not like and he can notice the same about you.
- Read erotic stories to each other and tell which ones you really like and why.

Remember that being a mother does not mean that you have to stop liking or enjoying sexual intimacy. Many women find that, as they grow older, their capacity to enjoy the full sensuality of intimacy actually grows.

You and your children

We have focused particularly on talking with your partner because he may be the support you need to implement the changes you want for yourself. However, your children are also part of that support, as well as being the ones who will benefit if you are happier, more self-assured and confident in your roles as a person and a mother.

Talking with your children is essential. Sharing what is important to them and what is important to you helps everyone understand each other and work towards these goals. The level of explanation varies with the child's age. However, even a young child can understand that you might want to be alone sometimes because it helps you "feel better".

One of the most important things to do when talking to children, no matter what their age, is to *listen*. Few adults actually listen to what their children are saying. Make sure that you understand the child's point of view (even if you disagree with it). It is okay to tell your child that you do not agree with him or her and that you have a different view.

Children are often placed in impossible situations by adults, particularly parents. They are often expected to know what is happening within their families without being told directly. If you expect changes to take place in your family as a result of talking with your partner and deciding on new priorities for yourself, tell your children. If they do not know what is happening, how can they help you? Some parents try to keep conflicts or difficult family news a secret from their sons and daughters. Most children will tell you that they have known when something was going on even if they did not know exactly what it was. This leads to worry in children – what they can imagine is often worse than the real news. If you are trying to change things – for instance, if you are trying to alter the balance of time that you and your partner spend with the children – tell them what is happening and why. This is not the time to moan about your partner but to talk about the positive benefits that everyone will gain from the change.

One way of enhancing the communication between you, your partner and your children is to hold a family meeting. Here are some guidelines:

- Ensure that everyone is present.
- One parent should take the lead to explain what the meeting is about. The message should be clear.
- The other parent may add something if he or she wishes.
- The children should be able to ask questions or make comments without being interrupted or criticized.
- The meeting should finish with a clear understanding of where the family as a whole is going.

A typical family meeting could discuss:

- the household chore rota with teenagers.
- what is happening to each of the children at school.
- the fact that the mother is going to spend some time away and how everyone else will need to help around the house.
- how both parents expect some privacy after 9pm.

Saying what you want: assertiveness

What do you want?

Do you really know what you want for yourself, or do you feel as if you have lost yourself over the years? If you could wish for anything at all, what would you want for yourself? If you had a few hours to yourself, what would you do with your time? At the moment, "going to sleep" might be one of the answers that runs through your mind. If this is so, you need more than ever to find some time for yourself. The exhaustion of trying to juggle too much at once is less a physical effect than an emotional one (except in those early months of a baby's life when no one seems to get enough sleep!).

What if you don't know what you want?

It may help to identify what you do *not* want. There may be some things about your day that are obviously stressful and which you would like to change. There may be some things that you are expected to do that leave you feeling resentful or frustrated. Monitor your daily life over approximately two weeks. Keep a diary in which you list the things you do and those that happen to you and how both leave you feeling.

This can take some effort because it is not enough to fill in the diary at the end of the day. Each change of activity and its effect on you needs to be recorded as it happens. This is a record of your feelings (*see* Diagram 6). After keeping this record for several weeks, you will be able to look for patterns, rather than just noting whether you had a good or bad day.

You may find that the same types of tasks or repeated contact with a particular person always leave you feeling stressed and low. Why is this? Ask yourself about why and how this happens. Do you need to change your relationship with this person or your approach to the task that distresses you? Will your partner help you change what is happening – or is he part of the problem? If you find that a friend, relative or partner is causing some of your stress, look at Chapter 15: *Talking together*. If it is the things you are expected to do day by day that stress you, start thinking about making changes. What would make your daily life better? Remember, if you do nothing, nothing will change for the better.

How to say what you want

Start by deciding what it is you want.

Be clear to others without being critical.

Ask those to whom you are talking to listen and not interrupt. Explain that talking to them may be hard for you to do and you would appreciate it if they would simply listen. Tell them that you do not expect them to *do* anything, just listen. Tell them that you do not expect any answers or solutions. You simply want to tell them how you feel and what you want.

Use "I" sentences.

- "I want to have more time to go out with my friends."
- "I need to get out of the house, sometimes on my own."
- "I would like to spend more time with you."

Times	Activity	How did it make you feel?
06.00		
07.00		
08.00		
09.00		
10.00		
11.00		
12.00		
13.00		
14.00		
15.00		
16.00		
17.00		
18.00		
19.00		
20.00		
21.00		
22.00		
23.00		
00.00		

Diagram 6   Daily diary to find out what you really want.

- "I enjoy my work and would like to aim towards a promotion."

As you talk, you might explain why you want these changes.

- "I'm having difficulty coping with the children as well as going to work."
- "I feel overwhelmed by all the demands on me and I need some help."
- "I've been feeling unhappy lately because we seem to be leading such separate lives."

How *not* to say what you want

- "You leave everything to me."
- "You never help with . . ."
- "You always come in and expect . . ."

These statements sound like personal attacks and will result in one thing – defensiveness in the person you want to listen to you. If you are addressing your partner, he will respond to these attacks by shutting off or retaliating. Whichever defensive strategy he uses, it does not help you or him. You want to speak so that you will be heard. You want to be listened to. If you want to be heard, you have to make the effort to make it safe for the listener.

If *you* feel unsafe because your partner, colleague or family member has shouted at you or made you feel threatened in the past, take this into account. Arrange to talk in a public place such as a restaurant. If things get heated, ensure that you do not return home to an unsafe atmosphere. If you often fear for your safety, seek help from a local women's aid organization, or persuade your partner to seek help with you from a counsellor.

Mixed messages

In an effort to remain polite and not hurt other people's feelings, women often give mixed messages. How often have you watched as a friend says to a troublesome boyfriend, "I don't want to see you any more," only to find that she follows this up with telephone calls and meetings? At first, it may seem understandable, but when the pattern repeats itself over and over, your patience may run out and you ask: "Why don't you just stop seeing him?"

When you are thinking about what to say, make sure that you are clear about what you want to say and that you mean it. If you want more help and support with childcare from your partner, you can't criticize him for everything he does just because it is not as you would do it! This sends a conflicting message:

Help me

versus

You can't do it right

If you want to work more hours or return to your career, you can't make finding alternative childcare impossible (because you feel guilty at leaving your child in someone else's care). The mixed message here is:

I want to work

versus

No one can look after the children as well as I can

If you ask to spend more time with your partner, you shouldn't also send the silent resentful message that you are too busy even to sit down in the evening with him.

Don't be diverted from what you want to say. Check that you are still talking about your message. It is all too easy to be diverted into old arguments. Take the following example:

Jenny: I want to be able to spend more time at . . .

Peter: But you said you wanted to stay at home with the children. How can you say this? Why can't you be happy at anything? You're always complaining.

Jenny: I'm not always complaining. That's not fair.

Peter: You're never happy. You're just like your mother. She never stops moaning.

Jenny: My mother isn't always moaning. Anyway, just listen to your mother . . .

What could Jenny have done to prevent this old argument? She could have told Peter that she had something to say and did not want to be interrupted. She could have told him that he could comment at the end. If Peter did interrupt with diverting comments, Jenny could have chosen not to respond to them – no matter what was said. Jenny should have returned to the message that she was trying to convey to Peter by saying: "What I'm saying is . . ."

Practise what you want to say

If you have friends who will help you, use them to practise being assertive. Say what it is you want to say and why. Say what you think you may have to change to get what you want. Think about what the person you are going to talk to might have to say – if you think you know, practise your replies.

If you do not have someone who can help, try sitting down opposite a pillow or chair and imagine that the pillow or chair is the person you want to talk to.

Learning how to talk together on a regular basis will help you feel safe to say what you feel and what you want. It will also teach your partner or family members to listen and to express their own feelings and wants in turn.

For practise, fill in the blanks in the following statements with some of your own thoughts:

Start with the things you want:

- I want to have more time to ....
- I want to do less of ....
- I need to ....
- I would like to ....
- .... makes me feel happy.
- .... is fun and I would like to find a way to do more of it.
- I enjoy ....
- I like ....

Now say what is difficult for you, makes you feel unhappy or stops you doing what you want to do:

- I am having difficulty coping with ....
- I feel overwhelmed by ....
- I have been feeling unhappy lately because ....
- I do not want to .... any more.
- I cannot continue ....

Above all, be clear. Decide what the message is you want to convey and stick to it. Do not be diverted into discussing peripheral issues. Do not give mixed messages.

15

Talking together

Talking with the important individuals in your life – your partner, family club members, friends and colleagues – on a regular basis about your daily lives will help all of you understand the pressures each are under. It will also help you find out what each one wants or hopes for in the future. Facing things together is much better than trying to cope alone.

Talking with your partner

Key points to discuss with your partner

Society makes the assumption that, once married, the man has a responsibility to care for the woman. We may have moved beyond the days when a man had to ask a woman's father for her hand in marriage, but the assumption that accompanied this act is still with us.

With many couples, there is also an assumption that the woman will care for the children while the man takes on responsibility for supporting them financially. However, this assumption – which may be adopted with no conscious decision to do so – can be the cause for a gulf to form between some couples because they have never discussed the matters that arise from it. The man may gradually come to resent the woman because, in his eyes, she has an easy life, staying at home, playing with the children and attending coffee mornings, while he toils at work. The woman, in turn, may see the man as escaping the mundane boredom of the home – at work, he can share conversations and go out to lunch. Resentments build and the once-loving couple find their lives becoming isolated from each other.

However, many couples find that a partnership, with roles more blended than in the past, is a far more successful mode of living. But if you want this for yourself, you and your partner must be clear about your individual responsibilities to each other, to your children and to the rest of your family.

- Talk together about what you expect from each other.
- How would you describe a good partnership?
- Who will contribute what to the partnership?
- What does being a good parent mean to each of you?
- Who will contribute what to parenthood?
- Review your partnership whenever there is a change – e.g. a new job, the children starting school, the children becoming teenagers, the children leaving home.

Find time to talk regularly

This is more difficult to do than it may at first seem, especially when you have children to care for. Make plans to meet with your partner, just as you would if you were meeting with friends. If you can find a babysitter, have some of these meetings over a meal at a restaurant or over a coffee in a café. If you have to stay at home, turn off the television (you wouldn't believe the number of people who talk while half-watching television!), take the telephone off the hook and avoid as many predictable interruptions as you can.

Take turns to talk about your daily life and how it makes you feel

There are important guidelines to follow if you are to communicate clearly. One of the first prerequisites of communication is silence. You need your partner to listen. You don't need him to interrupt while you are trying to talk about your feelings and what you want. Neither does he. It is often more important to listen than to come up with any solutions or suggestions to solve your loved one's difficulties. The Samaritans, the British suicide-prevention charity, have a saying: Don't just do something, sit there!

Here are some other important things to bear in mind:

- Talk about yourself only.
- Don't use your talk to make an attack on your partner (look again at Chapter 14: *Saying what you want*).
- Talk about how you spend your day.
- Talk about what you enjoy and what you do not like.
- Talk about the things that you find most difficult.

When you have finished, do not attempt to come up with answers or solutions. When you first carry out these exercises, it is best to meet again a few days or a week later so that you both have time to consider what the other has said and not respond too hastily. When you do meet again, ask each other: What would you like to change?

This might be the hardest part, particularly if you want things to change in a way that will affect your partner. Perhaps you want to go back to work. Perhaps you want to spend more time with your partner. Perhaps you want to give up work and stay at home with the children. Perhaps he wants to swap and stay home while you go to work. Whatever the proposals, these are the ones to consider. Look at them as problems to solve between you, not to fight over.

Tell your partner how he could help to make things better. This is not a time to complain about everything that has gone wrong in the past. Rather it is a time to work towards a better future.

Tell your partner how you might help to make things better for yourself – the things you want to change in your life, the way you behave or feel.

Remember: Be sure that you tell your partner how you might help make things better for him too!

Examine your attitudes towards parenthood

Look at what being a mother means to each of you. Examine your own expectations of being a mother. Where do these come from – your family club? How would you like to be? What do you think a mother should do for her children? What do you want your children to be like as adults? For this to happen, what do you need to teach your children?

Now look at what being a father means to each of you. Examine your own expectations of what being a father is. Where do these come from – your family club? How would you like a father to be? What do you think a father should do for his children? What do you want your children to be like as adults? For this to happen, what does their father need to teach them?

Ask yourself the following questions:

- Do you expect the mother to be caring and the father to be strict?
- Do you expect the mother to be strict and the father to be sympathetic to the children?

- Do you expect mothers and fathers to co-operate?
- Do you expect mothers and fathers to conspire with the children behind each other's back?
- How can you use the ideas in this book to raise children who, when they are old enough, are able to go out into the world alone?

If you can't bring yourself to talk

There are some people who cannot seem to get past the first hurdle of sharing their thoughts and concerns. Remember, if you are not sharing your needs and wants, it is likely that your partner feels unable to share his with you.

To get over this block, sit down and write your partner a letter.

- Start with the good things about your partner and the good things in your life.
- Talk about what you find difficult.
- Say that you want to tell him these things because you want to work together on them.
- Ask your partner what he might want to say to you.

If none of this works

If none of this feels as though it is working, you and your partner will undoubtedly be having difficulty communicating over some important issues. If this is the case, consider going to see a counsellor who specializes in couple counselling. It can be very helpful to have someone who is skilled at helping couples take you through the first steps towards communication. Don't make the mistake of thinking that going for help is a sign of failure. There are many happy couples who have stayed that way because they have sought help when they needed it rather than let feelings and misunderstandings reach crisis point.

However, if you feel that your relationship has broken down completely, have a look at Chapter 17: *Separation and divorce*.

Talking with your family club members

You do not have to feel uncomfortable because you are talking to members of your family club rather than friends. Whenever you are talking with family members, ask yourself if you would behave any differently with a good friend. If you feel less important when with certain family members, you will need to work on convincing yourself that you are an adult now. Remind yourself how you deal with friends and colleagues and try to act in the same way with family members such as your parents. Ask yourself if you are being treated in a way that you would never accept from anyone else. If you realize that you are still being treated as a "little girl", you will need to tackle this with your parents.

Talking with parents

Remember you are an adult, and expect to be treated as such by both sets of parents. This means that your opinions count as much as theirs. It means that saying "no" to parents is as acceptable as saying "yes". It also means that it is recognized that, as the parent of your children, you have the final say on how they are to be treated, not your parents.

If you find, like Anne in Chapter 7, that a perfectly reasonable request (such as not to give the children sweets) is dismissed or your opinion on an issue is mocked, your parents are not seeing you as equal. You will need to be clear with them about what you want.

Use the same techniques with parents as discussed in Chapter 14: *Saying what you want*.

Don't moan about your partner to your parents or his. You, your partner and your children are your prime concern and should have your first loyalty. Any problems you have are best dealt with by you, within the intimate family circle. Although you may seek advice from parents or other members of the family club, you need to consider it alongside other points of view. Remember, your parents are not impartial and may hold beliefs that could stop you changing things for the better. If they support you against your partner whenever you complain about him, this may make you feel better in the short term, but it also means that your partner will feel criticized and isolated from the family club. The energy spent moaning with family club members would be better spent making an effort to get closer to your partner.

Talking with his parents is not helpful either. Many women try to get their partner's parents to talk to him when things become difficult. However, his parents probably believe the same thing as your partner about various issues (where do you think he got it from?). Again, it is your partner you need to talk with and draw closer to, not his parents.

Do not allow your parents or his to moan about you, your partner or your children. It is not helpful to you to have any concerns or anxieties amplified by hearing someone else moan about your family. You are left feeling anxious and somehow responsible for putting things right. If a friend started to talk in this way, would you put up with it? If your answer is "no", you should do something about it. Say if you want to stop talking about a particular subject. Tell the parents that you do not want to discuss it. You do not have to feel uncomfortable because you are talking to parents rather than friends.

Talking with friends and colleagues

The same principles apply when talking with friends and colleagues as with anyone else. You need to be clear about what it is you are trying to say. Practise if you need to by deciding what message you want to get across.

Remember that you are an adult. You have the right to your own opinions. You have the right to say "yes" or "no" as you please. As an adult, you also have to take responsibility for your choices. If you upset a colleague or friend, ask yourself why. Did you behave inappropriately? Are you responsible for the upset, or are you being pressured by their tears or anger into agreeing to something that you do not want to do? Look at who owns the problem. Think about how you can talk together and how to say what you are trying to say.

Talking with your parents or friends should *never* be a substitute for talking with your partner. *Never* tell things to your parents or friends if that knowledge will make your partner uncomfortable. After all, you wouldn't like him to do the same to you.

To separate out what you as an adult mother believe from what you are expected to believe, reread Chapter 10: *What stops you from being who you want to be?*

16

Other people's reactions to your change

People do not like change.
Change is difficult.
Families will try to keep things the same.

These are all phrases used earlier in this book. None of us likes change for change's sake. If we do want change, we want it to be for the better, such as moving to a nicer house, getting a better job or changing our appearance so that we look better.

If we have decided to change ourselves, we are doing something that we believe will make things better for us. If, having thought about the issues raised in this book, you have decided to say what you want and have begun to work at being a visible adult mother, you will probably find that some of the people close to you will not like your changes. These people – whether your partner, members of your family club or even your children – will resist your changes at first simply because change makes them uncomfortable: this is not behaviour that they recognize and are familiar with. They are used to things as they have been, and any change you make will force changes on them, too, which can be upsetting.

If you are aware that others are likely to try to change you back to the way you used to be, this can help you keep to what you have decided to do. The pressure to change back will ease as the others get used to the "new you" and what you are trying to do. If you don't respond to the pressure, the most intense resistance to your changes will usually only last a few weeks.

Dismissing you

"That's stupid."
"You don't know what you are saying."
"Yeah, yeah, you've said all this before . . ."
"How can you say that when you have no idea . . ."

All of these phrases, and more, are intended to give you a clear message: you do not know what you are talking about.

Emotional blackmail

"If you carry on like this, I will be angry/ill/never speak to you again."
"You can't do that or you'll make things impossible for me."
"Your brother/grandmother/partner will never forgive you."
"How can you do this to your children?"
"How could you change so much?"
"Why are you doing this to everyone?"
"You're spoiling everything."

These sorts of things are said by others who use emotion in an attempt to force you to feel guilt. They are the same as "How can you go and enjoy yourself with your friends at Christmas and leave me here all alone . . ." People who use this form of blackmail try to arrange things so that your only choice will be the one that makes them feel comfortable. Your comfort and happiness do not matter.

151

You can recognize the work of the emotional blackmailer by your feelings of guilt. If you feel terribly guilty whenever you try to do what you want or find yourself always apologizing for not agreeing with someone else, you are being treated as though you are an invisible woman.

"You must be ill"

"You must be having a breakdown."
"You can't do that."
"You need to see someone/a psychiatrist/a counsellor who will talk some sense into you."

These sorts of things are said when others think that the only reason for the changes in you is because you are ill. This is another form of dismissal because it sends you the message: "You are only saying this because you are unwell." However, your need for change and your attempts at becoming more visible may be the most helpful, healthy things you have ever done.

Your partner's reluctance to change with you

If you have the support of your partner to make the changes that you have decided to make, you are already halfway there. When both of you are working together towards making both of your lives better and your relationship closer, you can deal with outside pressures more easily. However, for many women, their partner is one of the main factors in the struggle to become visible. The following are some of the things that partners reluctant to help have said:

• "I can never change."

- "I don't understand you."
- "I don't like what you're trying to do."

If you hear things like these, you have a choice. You can put your partner before yourself *or* you can decide that you need to make changes anyway. If you do decide to go ahead, try to make your message to your partner clear. Look at Chapter 14: *Saying what you want*, and also Chapter 15: *Talking together*. Remember that it is not true that someone "can never change", only that they choose not to.

If the difficulties between you persist for more than a few weeks, consider going to a relationship counsellor together. If your partner will not go with you, consider going alone to explore what is happening in the relationship that has led to him taking such a strong stand. This may help you decide what to do next.

Children's resistance to change

Take time to explain to your children that you want things to change around the house. Tailor your talk to how old the children are, and make it clear that the change will help everyone in the family.

This does not mean giving long, emotional explanations of how much everything tires you out or how unhappy you are or how difficult the children may have been in the past. It does mean saying that you will expect them to, say, carry out certain chores so that everyone is helping in the house. It does mean saying that, for example, dropping clothes all over the house is no longer acceptable behaviour, and they can choose to co-operate or forfeit the use of the television or computer or not have evenings out. Read Chapter 23: *Visible adult mothers, successful children*.

Unforeseen consequences

One of the most difficult consequences of your own change may be the negative effects it appears to have on someone else. It is not uncommon for another family club member or even a partner to become depressed or anxious as a reaction to changes in another. Once again, this shows how a change in one member of the family club can have a direct effect upon every other member even if that effect is not obvious. If you do notice this happening, remind yourself that to go back to the way things were means everyone but you will feel better. In most cases, the anxiety or depression in the other person is temporary, only lasting until the changes have come to be accepted, however grudgingly.

Remember Anne who realized that she was being overwhelmed by the demands of her mother-in-law Brenda? As Anne took more and more control of her own time, she felt much better. As she stopped mediating between her husband Thomas and his mother, she found the time and energy to focus on the things that she wanted to do for herself and her family. But as Anne felt better, Thomas became increasingly unhappy and depressed.

At first, Anne felt a mixture of guilt and concern. Often she was tempted to step in and support Thomas by taking over the contact with his mother once again. But she resisted and found other ways of supporting him without taking on his problems. She also spent time with him, listening to his worries. As the weeks passed, Thomas decided that he had to confront his mother and put a stop to the now-constant tearful telephone calls at work.

Anne had handed the problem between Thomas and his mother back to Thomas. As a result, he first felt the strain of his mother's demanding, manipulative behaviour. Then he did what he perhaps should have done many years before: he said, "Enough is enough," and told his mother that her constant crying would not make him do things for her.

Anne was able to support Thomas in his dealings with his mother. She was no longer taking on his problem. Instead they shared the problem together.

Of course, the next person to be affected by the changes Anne started was Thomas's mother. Within the family club, the effects of the changes rippled on, but at least now the problem was where it should have been in the first place – with Brenda who obviously had a need to control others. Her anxiety had affected not only her but Anne, Thomas and their children. Now Brenda's anxiety stayed with Brenda.

This sequence of other people feeling bad once you feel better is not uncommon. It is important to remember that, to make difficult changes, people have to feel unhappy first – otherwise why change anything?

Your right to change

It is important to remember that you are entitled to your own opinion, even if someone else does not agree with you or even understand what you mean. Look at Chapter 12: *The adult mother's charter*, as well as Chapter 14: *Saying what you want*. Restate what it is you want and how you feel. It may be hard to stand your ground, but constantly remind yourself what you have decided to do and why. If you find that you have been overwhelmed by comments from someone else, ask yourself why this person is so threatened by your change. See any resistance to your change that, this time, succeeds in stopping you as merely one small step backwards –when you are ready, you can try again. Next time, you will be more prepared for others' reactions.

17

Separation and divorce

Unfortunately, there are times when things do not work out the way we would like them to. Over half of all marriages now end in divorce, and many of those involve children. Although the emphasis of this book is on improving your visibility and relationship with your partner, there are times when this is impossible within your existing relationship. If you feel that your relationship has already broken down, you are faced with some difficult times ahead. When you find that things are too bad to continue, changing yourself into a visible woman and an adult mother becomes even more important.

Don't believe it!

Most women who are struggling with a deteriorating relationship with their partner are told, even if apparently in jest, things like "I won't let you have the children" or "If you ever leave, I'll make sure you don't get a penny."

Because most women who are mothers have made the children their priority rather than their career, they feel powerless when told things like this. After all, women still rarely earn as much as their male partners, and so one of the immediate effects of separation is a reduced lifestyle – for both the woman and her children.

In a troubled or dying relationship, the man may use his economic power, implying that he is the one in control of the finances because he earns the most. However, this is not true. With good legal advice, a woman will begin to realize that she is not powerless.

Remember that, as a couple, you both decided to build a home and have children. You contributed 50 per cent to his career, his promotion or the building of the family business by caring for those things that he did not choose or have time to do himself. Be assertive. Believe in yourself and your own contribution.

Beware of advice from friends and relatives who say, "Don't upset him or he'll fight you more" – you may end up as victim of his every mood. Your lawyer is the one with experience of this kind of situation. At one stage or other, most men try to control their "exes" choices or the way their "exes" behave by stopping child maintenance payments. Do *not* believe it will never happen to you.

Protect yourself if necessary

Trust your feelings if you are anxious about a possible outburst of temper or threat of violence. Your feelings and instincts should not be ignored even if you do not feel able to justify them in a logical fashion. The feelings are there for a reason.

If you are nervous or anxious, make sure that you speak to your partner about contentious issues with another adult present in the house. Alternatively, go somewhere public but neutral.

Never feel ashamed of being afraid. Details of a support group for women subject to domestic violence are given at the end of this book.

Seek legal advice

Find a lawyer who will understand your position as a mother and a female partner who needs to ensure that she is not disadvantaged in the future as she raises the children of the relationship.

I personally believe that women are better cared for by female lawyers who specialize in matrimonial and family matters. Unfortunately there are many stories of women who are treated as if they are invisible by male lawyers who believe they know all about women's difficulties but have never been on the receiving end themselves.

Do not use the family lawyer! At this time, you need representation that is exclusively for you. Your lawyer should not have a history of acting for both you and your partner or for your parents or other family members. Through the others, he or she may have formed personal preferences and opinions on what should happen between you and your soon-to-be ex-partner. (The same applies to accountants in these circumstances.)

Check your finances

Ensure that you have your own separate bank account and that any joint accounts you share with your partner cannot be emptied by him without your permission. There are many women who have found that, not only have their partners run off with other women, but all of the money from the joint accounts has gone with them. Speak with your bank to find out what their policy is on large withdrawals by one person.

You may find yourself at a distinct disadvantage with other types of joint accounts – for example, mortgage accounts. As it is often the higher wage earner (almost invariably the man) who is "first named" on a joint mortgage account, some lenders regard any second name (almost invariably the woman) as liable if there is money owed on the account but not entitled to information, interest owed or even company share dividends – these only go to the first named account holder. Contact your lender to confirm your position.

Your independent accountant and lawyer can help you with all these details.

Friends and family

If you do decide to separate from your partner, you may feel under pressure from friends and family to behave in a particular way. Look again at Chapter 3 on family clubs to help you explore whether the reactions you are seeing in others can be considered to be in your best interests or those of the family club.

Many friends find the break-up of a relationship threatening. It makes them feel vulnerable, as if separation were catching. They look again at their own relationships and wonder whether they will last. For some of your friends, this will draw them closer to their partners; for others, it will make them wonder if they are strong enough to make the same decision as you.

If you are the only couple in your family club that has separated after having children and is now facing divorce, other members may have difficulty in accepting or even recognizing your position. You may be told emphatically that you must work things out for the sake of the children. Again, check out Chapter 14: *Saying what you want*, and stick to your guns. As we saw in the last chapter, no one likes change, but everyone usually learns to accept it, even if it seems to take a long time.

PART THREE

Fertility, responsibility and work

18

Those fertility decisions

Having sex leads to babies. This is a truth we seem to have forgotten. Contraception, especially the use of the hormonal contraceptive pill for women, has changed everything. It is regarded by most women as a guaranteed way of avoiding conception – even if they miss one or two pills from the packet. Women have come to believe that they are in control of their own fertility. They think that they can control not only when they wish to remain infertile, but also exactly when they become pregnant.

However, it comes as a shock to many women when they are not pregnant within a month or two of ceasing to use contraception. It comes as an equal shock when a woman finds herself unexpectedly pregnant – even if contraception has been used inappropriately or not at all.

Many women feel that their choice of when they will become pregnant is dictated by someone else – that is, by members of the family club. Women commonly talk about how their husbands wanted another child so they had one despite their own reservations. They talk of how, because their husband or parent was so nasty to them, they had been forced to have an abortion – a decision they now regret.

These explanations hand over an immense amount of power to others, such as partners or parents, for the final fertility decision. The women themselves are unimportant in the decision-making process or they are invisible, with all the power residing within the family club. They are so accustomed to considering everyone else that they forget or are unaware of their own needs and the personal responsibility that one has for one's own fertility and the choices associated with it. This invisibility confers some benefits, such as not having to be responsible when difficult choices are made. It is easier to blame someone else than take responsibility for a difficult decision.

Abortion: a cause for distress and conflict

Karen is in her early 30s and married to Ted, an older man. He left his first wife to come live with her, and for about three years, they were blissfully happy. Later, after their first child was born, things were a little strained, but they seemed to cope. When their son was eight years old, Karen fell pregnant with their second child. (What an interesting phrase that is, "to fall", as if it is an accident!)

"Everything was wonderful until I became pregnant again. Then Ted changed. He said he didn't want any more children. He'd already had three with his ex-wife and he said he couldn't go through all that again. He said he liked us not having to always be running after children. After all, our son is becoming more independent and we can go out when we want to as he can stay over with friends. Ted likes going out to dinner in the evenings, going to the theatre or cinema. When we had our first child, he was reluctant but he accepted it. He said that having one would be manageable. However, he was very clear that he didn't want this baby, no matter what I wanted.

"I told him I wanted the baby, that I loved him and I couldn't see why we couldn't still be happy together, but he wouldn't listen. He just stopped talking to me.

"I couldn't bear to be without him. I didn't want to be alone again and I thought . . . well, I thought we would have another chance to have a baby later. Maybe he would change his mind. So I did it. I had an abortion. I didn't have any choice."

Of course, Karen felt guilty about "getting rid of the baby", but as she talked, she also became more and more angry at Ted. I asked her how much pressure she had felt to have the abortion.

"Oh, I couldn't believe how he acted towards me. It was as if I'd done something wrong! He saw my being pregnant as all my fault. You see, I was on the pill. I felt bloated and tearful and I thought it was the pill so I had considered stopping it. But I didn't – even though Ted doesn't believe me. I did miss one or two out of the packet that month, but I've done that before and nothing has happened. Ted wouldn't think of using a condom – he said it was my responsibility to take care of that sort of thing."

What did I hear in this woman's words? A common mixture of who was responsible for the current situation. Karen had not taken her contraceptive pill daily, but Ted was also distancing himself from any part in the pregnancy.

"It doesn't sound as though you and Ted agreed much about these sorts of things – like contraception and having children."

"No . . . well . . . we never talked about it much. I mean, Ted told me that he hated condoms and that was it. He sort of assumed that I'd be on the pill and I was. We didn't talk about children either. I knew that his leaving his wife and their children had been really difficult for him so I didn't want to pressure him at all. But I really wanted this baby. I really did and he wouldn't even listen. He wouldn't even think about it."

Karen and I talked at length over the coming weeks as we explored her deteriorating relationship with Ted. We also talked about her grief over the abortion. Karen began to recognize certain patterns in her relationship with Ted:

- They did not discuss difficult issues but made assumptions.
- Ted expected to get his own way.
- Karen gave in to him.
- Ted was not taking responsibility for his actions.
- Karen was not taking responsibility for her actions.

A woman's fertility is her responsibility

This may not be a popular view, particularly in these days of equality between the sexes, with men trying to be more empathic and understanding. However, it comes down to basic biology. The woman is the one with the uterus. It is her problem if she has an unplanned pregnancy. This is the harsh reality of life. She may be in a relationship where the man is supportive and shares in the decision-making and responsibility. But he has a choice: he can walk away or distance himself emotionally as Ted did. But the woman has the new life growing within her body and all the consequences of that fact. Her choices are limited: have the baby or have a termination. It's that simple. How the male partner reacts is a completely separate issue.

Karen chose to have the abortion rather than lose Ted. That was her choice. She wanted the baby for herself. She wanted to become a mother again. But more than wanting the baby, she wanted to keep Ted. This is the harsh truth, one that Karen was struggling with and one that led to feelings of guilt. Karen chose to get rid of the baby rather than lose Ted. The baby was not so important to her after all.

Karen and other women tussle with the issue of abortion for many reasons. Despite what many would have us believe, religion is rarely a cause. In the early days of a pregnancy, women are faced with the decision either to carry to term or to terminate. They know that to continue the pregnancy will change their lives for ever, whether they already have children or not. The moral and religious arguments may continue for all time, but when faced with a pregnancy that is unwanted, either by her or her partner, a woman has no time to consider anything but personal issues.

The struggle focuses most often on the relationship. The final choice is often regretted because the relationship that the woman is attempting to preserve may be irrevocably changed as a result of the pregnancy. We seldom hear of couples who trace the deterioration of their relationship to the conception of their children – but these couples are as common as those who resent each other for years because of conflict over abortion.

It doesn't have to be this way. The relationship between the woman and the man who choose to have a sexual relationship, so risking pregnancy, is blurred into a decision regarding an abortion. Karen came into therapy complaining that she had not wanted her abortion and that Ted had made her do it. This was not true, and both Karen and Ted were suffering as a result of this untruth. Whether you approve of Ted's silent withdrawal or not, he had made his position very clear to Karen. It was this clear expression of feeling that Karen was unable to handle:

"I hated him for not agreeing to let me have the baby. I wanted him to want another baby with me. I really did not get pregnant deliberately, although I suppose I had been a bit careless, missing some of the pills . . .

"I always thought that I would fall in love and marry. I was sure of it. I wanted a good marriage and lots of children. My parents were happy, and I wanted the same for myself. I wanted it all, but instead, here I am – I have just one child. I had an abortion."

Karen's sadness focused on differences between herself and Ted, which had been brought out into the open by the pregnancy. Karen wanted a husband and more children of her own. Ted did not want further children, and looked forward to them being simply a couple together as their son grew up and left home. Their ideas and responses to similar situations were very different because they came from very different personal and family backgrounds, or family clubs. They liked and loved each other, but what they wanted for themselves in the longer term appeared irreconcilable.

Over time, Karen was able to see that Ted had been nothing but honest with her once the pregnancy was discovered. He had not pretended that he did not mind about the baby and then left Karen six months later. Instead, he had stated his position and then had become quiet and withdrawn. Karen decided to talk with Ted about all that had happened between them instead of maintaining the uncomfortable silence they had established. When she returned to see me, she seemed very different.

"We talked for hours, even though it was very painful. It was the first time I had given him a chance to tell me how he felt. He is terribly broken up about it all. He feels guilty, too. I thought he didn't care before. Now I know he cares about me very much, but the pregnancy was something he couldn't cope with. He says he never wanted to pressure me into deciding either way, but it meant he couldn't say anything to me in the end. Because it would have been untrue, he couldn't tell me that he wanted me to have the baby. But, when I look back now, I realize that *that* was all I wanted to hear. I wouldn't listen to anything else. I wanted to make him want the baby. I tried to make him do what I wanted."

Now Karen and Ted could start to re-examine their relationship and its future. They had avoided what many couples face following an unplanned pregnancy – years of resentment that he had forced her to have the baby or have an abortion, and years of resentment that she had refused to see that he had a right to an opinion that differed from hers.

For instance, perhaps a husband says to his newly pregnant wife: "No, I don't want you to have a third child now. We're just getting past the nappy stage with the other two and just beginning to be able to travel again. This baby would put us back at the beginning, and on top of that, we can't afford another one."

What is a woman to do? If she has given up her job to stay at home to raise the children, she has no economic or financial security. If the breadwinner – the man with all the financial power as well as an emotional hold over her – says "no", it is understandable that she, like most women in this situation, will have an abortion even if it is not her first choice. If the woman works, the responsibility of raising all her children – including the new one – on her own may be too much for her to face even if she could survive financially. For these practical reasons, many women choose abortion. However, afterwards, the guilt and the resentment they feel equals or exceeds Karen's.

The women in this position feel that they had no choice. They want to be perfect mothers. They want to continue their pregnancies and not join those bad mothers who have abortions. But to go against their partners' wishes would, in their minds, have devastating consequences: the loss of their partners' love and so the possible loss of their perfect families; the loss of their partners' financial support; the loss of their home; the loss of everything for which they have already sacrificed their selves over the years.

However, the partners in this position also have feelings and choices in this, just as Ted had feelings about whether Karen should continue with her pregnancy. No decision is made that does not affect your partner.

Being pressured into having more children

Although it is not widely recognized, there is much pressure on women to have further children. Single children are still a rarity in our society. Why? The answers that women give often focus on the benefits for the first child (so he or she will have a brother or sister) or on a family truth (only children are usually spoilt). Once a woman has made the necessary changes in her life to accommodate the arrival of her first child, having another one or two is often perceived as not making much difference. This perception does not take into account the effect that each and every child has on the mother.

Having further children means having to plan out the children's various commitments as well as your own. A typical mother of several young children talks about the constant running from nursery school gate to school gate to work to afterschool clubs to children's birthday parties. Mothers of older children and teenagers find that the school gate is merely exchanged for the judo class, the local swimming pool, friends' homes.

What do you want? If it has always been your dream to have several or lots of children, you know what you want. As an adult mother, you will consider the implications of this decision on your life and take responsibility for them. As an adult mother, you will discuss the consequences of further children fully with your partner and work out a way of coping so that neither of you feels overwhelmed or invisible.

Decision-making as an adult mother

Any decision concerning fertility and having children should not be taken lightly. It helps to separate the decisions that have to be made into their rightful places.

The most important question is: What do you want for yourself?

Ask yourself what it is *you* want. Try to remove yourself from the comments and opinions of others such as partner, parents or friends. This decision will affect you for the rest of your life. To decide on a course of action simply because someone else will benefit only leads to resentment and difficulties later.

Common questions you (and your partner) should consider

- Do you want a baby, with all that entails? You will not just be having a baby, but will be committing yourself to a lifetime of caring for another human being.
- Do you want a baby so much that you would face this alone if your partner does not want another child? Is this what you would choose for yourself?
- How will your life change? If you have plans for the future embracing a career or other ambitions, consider what an effect having one child or more will have. Examine Chapters 19 and 20, on working mothers, to find out some of the conflicts that might arise.
- Do you see pregnancy as a means of fixing something within the relationship? Has it crossed your mind that this baby might make your partner settle down or stop you wanting to leave him or any other such thoughts? It will not work. A pregnancy and the strain of raising a child accentuate differences between people; they do not bring them together.
- Do you have the finances or time to support your child or children alone? If you don't, who do you expect to contribute?
- Do those people know that you may rely on them to support you and the baby financially or give of their time to babysit?

- Is this what you want from your partner?
- If you already have children, how will your having another baby affect their lives – for better or worse?
- How will having another baby affect your partner's plans for the future?

The decision to continue with a pregnancy commits you to being a mother to that child for the rest of your life. If we want to be taken seriously, if we want to be treated as people in our own right, we have to take responsibility for our choices. We make our own choices, take our own risks and live with the consequences.

Questions to discuss with your partner

- Who will take care of the child?
- Will your partner make allowances for your change in circumstance?
- Will you and your partner renegotiate roles and responsibilities?
- If you are employed outside the home, how will you balance the extra responsibility of the next child?
- Can you afford the extra expense and, possibly, the loss of income due to a reduction in work hours?

19

Working mothers

All mothers are working mothers. The women who choose to remain at home looking after their children full time while their partners work are also working – full time. The fact that society does not always recognize this does not mean it is not true.

It helps to see the couple as a team. If one person, either the mother or the father, works long hours, he or she should remember that, without the "stay at home" parent, the "working" parent would not be able to commit so much to the job.

This chapter looks at the difficulties of those employed outside the home. The problems of these working mothers are unique because it seems impossible to balance the role of good employee and perfect mother.

Walking the tightrope

Mothers in paid employment feel that they cannot win. They attempt to balance the demands of motherhood with the demands of their employers. The working woman walks a tightrope. Wobble a little too far on one side – by attempting to earn much-needed money to maintain the family or to focus on her own career – and she is accused of neglecting her children and being a bad mother. Wobble too far to the other side and she is a bad employee. She is destined to walk this tightrope for as long as she tries to be perfect.

The needs of both the job and the children change throughout the year, sometimes every week. It is the rare woman who feels that she has the balance right. Indeed, the woman who says that all is well one week may find everything tumbling round her ears the next.

This balancing act begins with the decision to have a child. With the availability of contraception and abortion (discussed in the previous chapter), I am assuming that a working woman who proceeds with a pregnancy is actively choosing to become a mother. Laws have been passed to protect the positions of women if they become pregnant while employed. Women are generally given the right to maternity leave and to return to the same position within the company once the maternity leave is over. Is it as simple as this?

In many professions, the senior managers and directors are mostly men. At the same time, in some of these professions the greatest number of employees are women. Is this just a coincidence?

We women take the main responsibility for raising our children often without thinking or making an informed, conscious choice.

New mothers but old colleagues: Lynne's return to work

"I don't know what's gone wrong. I thought everything was going to work out well. I was so pleased when Paul and I decided to start a family and couldn't believe it when I fell pregnant so quickly. Everyone in my team at work was so pleased for us. We're a close team. We have to be as we work hard and have to support each other. But since I returned from having Alice, I feel that the other members of the team haven't got time for me. If I talk about Alice, they look bored and change the subject. Everything seems to have changed. I've thought of leaving work, but Paul and I can't afford it. I have to work but maybe I should find another job. I just don't know what to do. It all seems so unfair."

Lynne spoke of the changes that had taken place in her life over the past year and a half. She had changed from being a working woman within a young married couple to being a working mother with a family. This was a struggle for Lynne as she tried to be a perfect mother to her daughter Alice, a good wife to Paul and a good member of the team at work. Not surprisingly, she found it all too much to cope with and was wondering what to do next. Lynne's immediate thought was to find a new job, but further discussion showed that she was likely to take the same problems with her to her next one. It was Lynne's struggle to balance both work and her role as parent that had resulted in these conflicts.

As we talked, it became clear that Lynne's relationship with her work team had deteriorated since her return. I asked Lynne if there could be any reason for this.

"Well, I suppose there is. You see, if I'm off work, my workload has to be shared among the rest of the group, which consists of only six people. When I took maternity leave, there was a big project on and no one was taken on to replace me temporarily. It meant that, for the busiest time of the year, there were only five people doing the work of six. I heard afterwards that Helen ended up taking three weeks off because of the stress. I think they blame me, even though it had nothing to do with me. Helen has been very cold towards me for the last year."

Lynne had never considered the implications of her pregnancy on the people she worked alongside. Her personal decision to have a child affected each and every member of her team. Helen, in particular, found the strain of carrying the extra load at this busy time of year unbearable. Her health had deteriorated and she blamed Lynne for her difficulties. Lynne had been so concerned with how Alice would be without her once she returned to work that it had not occurred to her that her colleagues might have their own problems.

The employment realities of being a working mother

Employment legislation recognizes that it is the woman who has a uterus and bears children for herself, for her partner and for society as a whole. However, it does seem naïve to take extended leave and not expect it to affect our chances of promotion and our relationships with other colleagues. After all, our colleagues and our employer do not expect to be socially responsible for us.

It is this contradiction between the expectations of family and society that women employees deal with daily. As responsible adult mothers, we need to recognize the contradiction in order not to be overwhelmed or victimized by it. If a company's main objective is to make money, a female employee who chooses to have a baby while in its employ will cost it money. It may take some time after the period of maternity leave for the woman to prove herself "reliable" once again in an employer's mind. Your employer and your colleagues are human and are affected by the extra effort they have to make because of your personal decision to have a child.

As adults we need to recognize the effects of our personal decisions on others and be prepared to take responsibility for our choices. We make these decisions often knowing that employers and society as a whole are not supportive of working mothers.

Trying to walk the tightrope

Lynne continued to look at the effect on her team of her personal choice to become a mother:

"I've had quite a bit of time off over the past few months. Alice has had a couple of colds, nothing major, but Paul and I felt she shouldn't go to daycare. I also get to work late sometimes because Alice hates it when I drop her off at daycare and I have to hold her until she settles. The daycare staff are very good but it makes me late . . ."

Lynne paused, looking thoughtful before saying: "I've caused quite a big change in the team, haven't I?"

"The changes caused by your having a baby seem to have spilled over into the team, haven't they?" I suggested. "Perhaps this is why the others have changed towards you. Is there anything you can do now to make things better?"

"I don't know what to do. I could speak to them and tell them that I realize how much they had to do while I was away. I could tell them that I had no idea how much it would affect everyone. But what am I supposed to do – never have children?"

With this question, Lynne is voicing the impossible truth. The choices that women face as a result of their biology need to be recognized by all. The woman who chooses to become a mother and also work becomes, by default, a bad employee and bad mother. The root of this, however, does not lie in biology or in the woman's abilities, but in the invisible status that mothers assume. Once the birth is over, shouldn't the woman be able to expect to share the load of childcare with her partner?

"I never thought it would be so bad. I thought Paul would share the load with me. He said he would help to care for Alice, but it hasn't worked out that way. He gets home later than I do because he travels an hour to and from work, so I have to pick up Alice from the daycare centre and take her home. I feed her and bathe her before Paul gets home. If she's sick, I have to look after her, not Paul. Then at the weekends, he plays football with his friends because he says he needs to relax."

"Have you told Paul that this is how you feel?"

"No . . . I feel it's me not coping, not him. And you'll never believe it – he wants to start planning having another one! He wants more children already."

Lynne found herself resented by colleagues at work and she in turn resents Paul for not being as involved with caring for Alice as she had been led to expect. She has let things continue this way because she did not tell Paul how she really felt, and she hadn't really done anything to find out what the problem was at her workplace. Both Lynne and Paul started with the best of intentions, but both have fallen into the trap of assuming that things would work out as long as they just keep trying hard. Lynne wants to stop feeling that everything is out of her control. If she leaves things as they are, her resentment may build and affect her relationship with both Paul and Alice. Lynne is becoming invisible as she tries to do everything. The more she succeeds in balancing her job and motherhood, the more invisible she becomes as her own needs disappear from view.

To change things, Lynne will have to voice her own needs clearly and stop being invisible to those around her. She is in danger of falling into another trap: being visible to others only when she is seen as a bad mother and bad employee. She can choose to share her frustrations with Paul and see if the two of them are able to work out a way of sharing the load of caring for Alice more evenly. It is only in failure that Lynne (and her needs) became visible and her difficulties began to be addressed.

What about the father?

Of course, it is easy to say that the father should take on half the responsibility of parenting. Many new mothers start with this aim in mind. However, reality develops differently as women settle into the role of motherhood and, with it, invisibility. Any feelings of being overloaded are counter to their desire to be perfect mothers.

Meanwhile, the fathers may feel an increased sense of responsibility for the financial support of their new families. Instead of being more available to care for the practical needs of their children and emotionally supportive to their partners, they may become even less available as they work longer hours. The combination of these stereotypical gender roles is a recipe for disaster, both for couples' relationships and for women's future in the workplace.

Couples who address these issues together have a better understanding of each other's pressures and needs and so can support each other. More of a problem is how to change the bias in the treatment of mothers and fathers at work. If a woman says that she has to take time off to care for a sick infant, the employer will sigh but reluctantly accept this as a penalty for employing mothers. If a father says that he has to take time off to care for a sick infant, the response is likely to be: "Why can't your wife do it?" Until this disparity of treatment is challenged, the struggles of working mothers and fathers will continue.

20

Practical steps for working mothers

Questions to consider

What can you manage?

Are you simply trying to do too much? Many working mothers suffer most because they are spending all their energy reaching for unattainable goals. This does not mean that women should not be ambitious, but rather women should be ambitious for those things that are possible.

How much practical help can you rely on from others?

Are you on your own or do you have support? One of the greatest struggles for working mothers is relying on someone who regularly lets them down. If you have a partner who talks about sharing child care but, in reality, is always too busy or not available, you need to recognize this instead of continuing to fool yourself. It is easier to cope when you know that you have to cope alone than trying to share the load with someone who is constantly unavailable.

Look at childcare realistically. Take into account the obvious things, such as cost and the suitability of the carer. Many women also learn the hard way the importance of flexibility in childcare arrangements if they have to work late, if their child is sick, etc. Another consideration is how much time per week it takes to travel from your home to the childcarer and then on to work. Are your arrangements practical? For example, do you set out in the opposite direction from your workplace to travel 30 minutes to your childcarer? Do you realize that this adds up to two hours of travel to your journey every day (30 minutes x 2 x 2)?

How flexible are your working conditions?

It makes a difference if your employer will accept variations in the time you arrive and leave work. If your employer depends on you to be at work at a specific time every day, this, too, has to be considered when selecting childcare.

How much consideration should you actually expect from your employer?

This is one of those impossible questions! Many employers are criticized because they make it difficult for mothers to take time off when they need to care for their children. However, the employer has a business to run, and recognizing this may help you in your negotiations with him or her. Can you negotiate an exchange of time – offering to make up time missed, for example?

Would some changes make your dual role easier?

There are some changes that may make being a working mother easier. For example, moving closer to your workplace may not appeal to you initially, but think about it. The amount of time spent travelling to and from home to childcare to work takes up many hours a week for some women. Those extra hours could make a big difference to you. Spend some time thinking about how you would like things to be. What do you want? Even a few small changes might make a difference.

Points to remember

- Don't try to be the perfect employee – no one is.
- Don't try to be the perfect mother – no one can be.
- Don't feel guilt every time you have to say "no" – recognize why you need to say "no" and believe in yourself.

Mothers in part-time work: Diana's story

Diana is in her late 30s and has two teenage children. She works for a local company in a secure part-time job. Her husband James is employed full time in a very demanding managerial position in a large international bank.

"I had to have a couple of weeks off about a year ago. I felt exhausted. I had a virus and couldn't shake it off. I was so tired. Everyone was wonderful, especially my mother. She came down and stayed with us, took care of the children, cooked and cleaned and simply left me alone to rest. I hadn't had a day – let alone two weeks – like that for years . . . probably not since the children were born.

"I went back to work feeling much better. I thought that I'd completely recovered and did very well at work, but now I am off again. My doctor told me to stay home for a week. She also suggested that I come to see you while I was off work. I'm feeling so tired and I know why: I did what I always do, I took on too much at work. So what do I do now?"

I suggested that we look at the various pressures on Diana's life, starting with work.

"My job is part time, three days a week. I've been there for about ten years now, ever since the children started school, and although the job has changed over the years, I do enjoy it. I spend my time promoting the company's products to other businesses. There are three of us in the team and I'm the only part timer. I know what I do – I take on more and more until I feel as though I am running in circles. Then I have one of these spells where I can't get out of bed."

"So when you feel that you can't cope any more, your body announces it's had enough and you're ill in bed?" I asked. "It sounds as though taking to your bed is the only way you ever get to be looked after by someone else."

"You're right. Unless I'm ill, I'm the one who keeps everything going at home. I have to be dying before the children would think about cooking their own meals. James likes the house to be tidy and ordered when he gets home or he gets all grumpy. I understand why when he works such long hours, but it means that, on the days I work, I have to get home and tidy everything up from the children before he walks in the door. When my mother came to stay and took over, I couldn't believe how much help it was. I don't know what I would have done without her for those two weeks – dragged myself out of bed, I suppose."

Here was the heart of the problem Diana faced. Even when we started talking about difficulties at work, the difficulties at home kept intruding. Was Diana trying to be all things to all people and all places?

Diana's voice was tinged with anger as she spoke of her family: "I pick up after the children. What do I mean, 'children'? They're 19 and 15! The oldest one has left school and taken a year out before going off to college. I thought she was going to travel or work, but instead she lies around the house watching television. The 15-year-old is studying hard for her exams. Well, she's supposed to be, but she finds time to go out with her friends and spends hours on the telephone. The girls simply drop their clothes on the floor in their rooms when they take them off at night. I spend all my time collecting dirty washing, cleaning dirty plates and transporting the girls around town."

I knew that I was listening to a woman who was trying hard to be the perfect mother and, I suspected, the perfect employee. "What about at work?" I asked.

"I try to be organized. I like to be seen to be good at what I do, but I don't feel as if I should have the responsible position I have."

"What do you mean, you don't feel you should have your position?"

"I haven't got the qualifications that the others in my office have. Whenever I finish a project and hand it over to my manager, I hold my breath, waiting for him to find out that I can't do my job."

"How long have you been doing this job?"

"Ten years."

"Did they appoint you knowing all about your skills and past employment record?"

"Yes."

"How long will it take for you to relax and realize that they think you do your job well? After all, they have been watching you do it for ten years now!"

Diana is attempting the impossible at work and at home. Why? She has fallen into the trap that many working mothers find themselves tangled in when trying not to be seen as bad mothers. She is trying to be both a perfect mother and a good employee, so failing to recognize the need to say "no".

Diana never thinks of herself. She acts as if she is both a full-time mother and a full-time employee. In her efforts to be perfect, she exhausts herself. To avoid saying "no" and upsetting anyone, she has to collapse into her bed, sick, to escape the responsibilities of both home and work. It is an interesting irony that, in order not to let anyone down, Diana drives herself until she cannot work or be a mother, but the only person available to look after her is her own mother.

When Diana's mother comes to take care of her, to support her by cooking meals and doing the laundry, she is giving Diana a much needed rest. But, despite the obvious immediate benefits, this act of kindness from her mother is actually preventing any constructive change.

Think back to the ideas discussed in Chapter 3 on families as family clubs that want to remain the same. Diana's mother is actually preventing everything in Diana's homelife from collapsing. Diana's role as cook and laundress has been taken over by her mother so that the household can continue to run smoothly. Neither the children nor the husband have to think about taking some of the burdens from Diana's shoulders. Their lives are not substantially affected by Diana being overwhelmed. The family members continue without change because they do not *have* to change. The family club continues unaltered and fundamentally undisturbed. Diana rests while her mother helps so that she can recover and return to the invisible and impossible position that drove her to exhaustion in the first place.

Diana is invisible to her family. When she was pregnant with their first child, she and her husband agreed that she would take on the household responsibilities and the care of the children. However, over the years, they have never re-examined this agreement as circumstances changed. Diana returned to work, but the responsibilities for the children and the household remained hers alone. As the children grew older, there was no reorganisation of chores so that the children could take over some of the responsibility for looking after themselves.

It is time for Diana and her husband to sit down and renegotiate their respective roles – see Chapter 21 for useful tips
on renegotiation and review. Using the steps described in
Chapter 14: *Saying what you want* and Chapter 15: *Talking
together*, they can arrange for a more even sharing of family
responsibilities.

21

New mothers returning to work

Why are you returning to work?

Are you returning or going to work because this is what you want to do? Think carefully about what you want for yourself. Ask yourself the following questions:

- What do you want for yourself?
- Are you simply doing something because you have never considered anything else?
- When you make your choice, are you avoiding comments and criticism?
- Are you pleasing someone else or trying to keep them happy by making a certain choice?
- Are you trying to stop them from getting angry when you make your choice?

If you are not used to it, it takes time and a lot of thought to decide what you might want for yourself. If you find that your answer is different from the plans you've already made, ask yourself why. Does being a modern woman mean to you that you *have* to return to work? Are you simply reacting to one of society's truths – that, if you are a particular kind of woman, you must decide this way?

Talk your ideas and thoughts through with someone. It always helps to say out loud what you are thinking. It forces you to order your thoughts so that someone else can understand them. Find a friend who will listen and not judge your decisions as right or wrong. Spend an evening talking through how you feel and how your partner or family might react to your decision about staying at home or returning to work.

Are you returning to work for financial reasons?

Ask yourself these questions:
- What do you want for yourself?
- What would you do if you had the choice?
- Do you feel angry with your partner or anyone else because you cannot stay at home?
- Is this fair?
- Should you expect someone else to be solely financially responsible for you and your baby?

Even if you are returning to work because you have to financially, it is worth looking at what your choice would have been if you had been given the circumstances in which to make one. It is too easy to blame difficulties with childcare or work – the tiredness and struggles – on having to work.

If you are returning to work because you have to financially, recognize the realities of your situation. You have responsibilities to yourself and your baby. (Look again at Chapter 18: *Those fertility decisions*.) One of those responsibilities is to be able to support yourself financially. It is no one else's responsibility to house and clothe you or your baby. If the father is not taking any financial responsibility for the baby, is there anything you can do about this? (See Chapter 14: *Saying what you want*.)

If you feel resentment or guilt at having to return to work, take time to look at your family rules and family truths. Look at the diagrams in Chapters 9–11. It is easy to feel guilty that you are not being a proper mother, but this is not automatically true.

Are you going to return full time or part time?

Ask yourself the following questions:

- What do you want for yourself?
- If you return to work full time, will you also be expected to take on the majority of the childcare? Talk with your partner about what will happen if . . .? Who will do what if . . .? If you are returning to work full time and your partner also works full time, do you regard each other as equals? If either of you answers "no" or acts as if the answer is "no", then ask yourselves: why not? Does he earn more than you? Men often do. Does this mean that your hours do not count as much as his? Do you agree with this?
- What can you and your partner do to share the responsibilities for both working and looking after your child?

This last question can have many answers. Talk with your partner – do not assume anything. Check regularly whether the situation is changing and one person is taking on more responsibilities than the other. Recognize natural talents and use them. For example, if you enjoy cooking, take that on as your job – but make sure that your partner does something equally time-consuming. Recognize that activities involving the baby – sitting and playing with him or her, bathing, putting to bed – are also "chores" and should never be regarded as "time off"!

If you are returning part time after you were previously full time, be careful that you are not expected by colleagues, your employer or even yourself to have full-time responsibilities on part-time hours (and pay). It is easy to slip into this if you are trying to please everyone. It is important to ensure that you remain visible, especially to yourself. If you feel like a full-time employee who is leaving a few hours early every day, you will soon start to feel guilty. Equally, if you see yourself returning as a part-timer who shouldn't be expected to do very much, you are likely to feel a burden to your other colleagues. Examine what you want and how you will feel about being part time, especially if you have always worked full time before the baby arrived. A person with clearly understood and agreed hours and responsibilities is likely to be happier and more successful.

What does your partner expect of you?

Does your partner expect you to take the main responsibility for the baby? With most couples, it does seem to be the woman who takes on the care of the children. This may result in your own ambitions and needs becoming secondary to everyone else's. Try not to allow yourself to become invisible. Women are raised with the idea that mothers give unconditionally – and this unconditional giving seems to spread to encompass all members of the family and even friends.

Find out as much as you can about what your partner expects of you. From this information, you can decide whether this is how you thought it would be. Then tell your partner what you expect of yourself.

This is a good time for you and your partner to develop your own unique set of family rules. Look at the family diagram (page 108) that you completed and see if you can identify the family rules and family truths that you inherited from the families you both came from. Remember, you are an adult now and have a family of your own. You can now create your own family rules.

What does your family expect of you?

This is an important time to examine the history of your family. What are the women in your family like? What have they expected out of life? What are the men in the family like? What have they expected out of life? Do you come from a traditional family? How will this affect what you are expected to do at home? Take time to follow the guidelines on family diagrams in Chapter 10.

Once you look very clearly at your respective families, you should be more able to see unspoken family rules. Is it a family rule that the women take total care of the children? Is it a family rule that fathers should remain distant from their children? Is it a family rule that one partner has to be dominated by the other?

But do you have to follow these family rules? You have the power to decide against them. You and your partner can say: "We want things to be different." Talking about what others have always taken for granted means that you are not blindly following family rules without even being aware of their influence.

Talking with your partner

Talking with your partner on a regular basis about your daily lives helps both of you understand the pressures you are both under. It also helps both of you to appreciate what the other wants or hopes for in the future. Facing things together is much better than trying to cope alone. Look at Chapter 15: *Talking together*.

Some of the topics to discuss when talking together will probably be:

- How has becoming a parent affected each of you?
- What are the extra pressures you feel now that you are parents?
- What are your worries about returning to work?
- How will your returning to work affect both of you?
- How will returning to work affect the baby?
- What are the positive things that can come from returning to work?
- Who may try to influence your decision or make negative comments about your choices?
- How will you deal with this?

Make sure your partner knows that things will be different for him once you start work. One of the danger times in a changing relationship is when a woman returns to work after giving birth. When she temporarily leaves work towards the end of pregnancy, the woman usually takes over looking after the household chores, and when the baby arrives, she carries on. Meanwhile, her partner continues to work full time, and gradually the traditional roles of husband as supporter and wife as housekeeper and mother are established.

Even though it may be only a few weeks or months before the woman returns to work, this pattern often echoes the roles with which the male partner is already comfortable, including the idea of woman as mother. His lover is now a mother and the feelings and expectations between the couple may change. When the woman attempts to return to work, the duties of caring for the baby, arranging childcare, and maintaining the household remain with her. Her role as working woman has become invisible. The male partner continues with his role of working full time to support the family, without a thought as to how the woman has now acquired extra responsibilities.

Arranging childcare

This issue is a fraught one for new parents. You may have the natural worry about choosing the wrong care. This concern may be heightened if you are feeling guilty about leaving your baby with someone else. Here are some tips that may make things easier:

- Preferably use someone recommended to you by another mother.
- Trust your instincts – your unconscious may be sensing something important. Don't ignore it.
- Ensure that your childminder knows your hours clearly before you start work.
- Find out how flexible the childminder will be if you have to work late or start early.
- Speak to other parents who use the same childminder.

Consider using registered childminders rather than family or friends. At first sight, using members of your family for childcare may seem the perfect solution. All the guilt at "leaving baby with a stranger" disappears when you think of leaving your baby with your own mother or his. But this "perfect" solution is always fraught with problems. Unlike a childminder, whom you can hire or fire, it is difficult to complain to your own mother or sister if she doesn't do things the way you want. It is also likely that your own mother or mother-in-law will feel that she knows more than you about looking after children – after all, she already raised you or your partner! This puts you in an unwinnable position, where you are unable to develop the confidence or even the skills to become a confident mother in your own right. All the family truths may exert themselves to make you feel like an inadequate mother who should not be working.

If you do have to use a family member or friend for childcare, keep the following in mind:

- Do not allow childcare to become a favour that has to be paid back.
- Consider paying for the service, no matter how little, so that you can keep everything on a business-like basis.
- Write up an agreement just as you would for formal childcare.
- Agree on hours and flexibility just like formal childcare.
- Remember, you are the mother of your child; no one else is.

Talking with your work colleagues

Remember what happened to Lynne when she returned to work? Without realizing it, she was allowing resentment towards her to build up among her colleagues. When you return to work, talk to those people you work closely with about what has happened while you have been on maternity leave. Be especially careful to find out about the effect that your absence has had on others.

- Find out if there have been any difficulties.
- Find out what changes have taken place.
- Find out who has fallen out with whom and who is now close to whom so you don't make inadvertent mistakes.
- Take some of your closest colleagues out for lunch away from the office so you can chat.
- Find out who else is in the same position as you as employee and new mother. Meet up and compare notes on how to manage!

- Don't spend all your time at work talking about your baby. Of course, you love your baby, but no one else is as interested as you are!

You should also talk with your bosses about your work arrangements. You are no longer the same employee they knew before your baby was born. You have new responsibilities at home, and the experience of becoming a mother will have changed you personally.

- Find out exactly what your boss expects of you, especially if your hours are now reduced.
- Voice any concerns if you are working (and being paid for) fewer hours but you are still being expected to do the same amount of work as you did when full time.
- Your boss may not know you are committed to returning to work – so say so!

Recognize your own limitations

You are not superwoman! You have changed and your priorities may have changed as well. You will never be the perfect mother and you will never be the perfect employee because no one can be. Instead you are trying to balance everything. If things get difficult, say so. If you say nothing through a misplaced sense of failure or guilt, you are making yourself invisible. If you struggle on, you are likely to crumble and not be able to manage anything. Instead, recognize your own stress when you feel it. Acknowledge any feelings of guilt and identify where they come from. Are they your own misgivings, or are they from family truths? Are you being expected to manage more than you should?

Over the years, mothers who work begin to realize how they have to be simply "good enough". If you recognize the impossibility of your situation, you can stop trying so hard to be the perfect mother and perfect employee. You might focus instead on what you can achieve and accomplish – what is important to you.

Renegotiation and review

Review your own situation regularly. Whenever there is a change, such as a new job for either you or your partner, a child starting a new school, the children becoming teenagers or leaving home, make sure you look at how this will affect you and your partner.

- Talk together about what you expect from each other as things change.
- Who will contribute what to the partnership after these changes?
- What does being a good parent mean to each of you? This will change over the years so this question needs to be asked again and again.
- What does doing well at work mean to each of you? How important is it now?
- Look over the suggestions for new mothers returning to work earlier in this chapter and think about how they may still apply to you.
- If you were starting over again as working mother, would you do things differently?
- If the answer is "yes", is there anything you can change now that will help make things better?
- Would your partner do things differently if given the chance?
- Are you trying to be the perfect mother and employee?
- Recognize that you have needs of your own.

New mothers returning to work

- Start to say what you want from others.
- Start to say "no" when you are being asked to do too much.
- Stop blaming others and start changing things for yourself.
- Insist that older children act like the almost adults they are.
- When necessary, renegotiate your agreement regarding the household and childcare.
- Stop feeling guilty!

22

Single motherhood

Having a baby on your own is a difficult situation to be in. No matter how hard you may have thought about this, whether the pregnancy was planned or not, the realities of being a single mother only strike you once you have had the baby.

Single motherhood has become more a matter of choice than mistake and needs to be recognized as such. This does not mean women without partners are not subject to the difficulties described and solutions proposed in this book. Indeed the single mother is as vulnerable to the influence of the family club, family rules and absolute truths as any one else. Why should she be an exception? Take the story of Gayle.

Gayle's story

After working for over ten years, Gayle started to feel that there must be something more to life. She had been in several long-term relationships, but none of them had resulted in what she really wanted: marriage and a family of her own.

As Gayle approached 30, she started to panic. Her job was okay but it did not give her the satisfaction it once had. Had she been "left on the shelf" as far as men were concerned? Certainly Gayle's mother thought so. Every time Gayle spoke to her on the telephone, her mother asked whether there was a new man in her life. She would always talk about Gayle's sister who was married and had two children. Before they said goodbye, Gayle's mother always said that all she wanted was for Gayle to be happy like her sister.

Then Gayle met someone she felt close to, but both of them had been hurt before and neither wanted to rush into marriage. They retained their separate homes, preferring to keep the freshness in the relationship rather than sharing washing and cleaning chores. Gayle wanted a baby and decided that, if her partner was willing, she would go ahead – even if he decided not to stay with her later. Of course, Gayle's family was confused. They assumed that there would be a hurried marriage – there was not. They assumed that Gayle was upset – she was not – and that this pregnancy was a mistake –it was not.

Gayle sailed through her pregnancy and, after her maternity leave, returned to work. In her usual fashion, she was organized, found good childcare and seemed to balance everything, much to everyone's admiration.

It was at this point that Gayle came for help because, despite outward appearances, she was desperately unhappy. She described a feeling of constant inadequacy and worried about the effects that not having a father living in the house would have on her adored baby son Sam.

"How is he going to feel when he doesn't have a dad to go out to play in the park at weekends? I wonder now if I should ever have had him, even though I love him so much."

We started by looking at where these worries were coming from. It quickly became obvious that Gayle's unhappiness was worse at weekends and got better as the week went on. She had assumed that this was because she was at work during the week but often alone with her son Sam at weekends. As we talked, it became clear to Gayle that she was very happy looking after Sam and sharing time with his father. The gloom and doom overcame her on Sunday evenings. Why? Just like Anne in Chapter 7, it was the telephone call from the family that influenced Gayle's mood.

What was happening here?

Even though Gayle lives far from her parents and sister, their beliefs and the values of the family club invaded her life every Sunday:

- Gayle's parents held her sister up as the perfect example of what was expected.
- Gayle's family club had never contained a single mother.
- The family club expected mothers to stay at home with their children, not work.
- Gayle did not feel able to challenge the assumptions of the family club.
- Gayle did not know how to talk with her family about her life and choices.

Gayle was left feeling inadequate because she was not conforming to the family club expectations. She needed to spend some time thinking about her own values and her own rules, as well as recognizing the family club rules that were influencing her feelings. She went through the steps described in Part Two concerning family truths and talking together with family.

Several months later, I saw a very different Gayle. She walked confidently into my office and told me how much better she was feeling about herself. In recognizing how destructive the Sunday telephone call was to her, Gayle had examined her own family club. Asking herself the questions "What do I want?" and "What do I believe?", she was able to decide what she believed herself and what was important to her.

"Derek, Sam's father, and I are getting on better than ever now. We know that we don't want to live together or even have an intimate relationship, but he's a good father to Sam. He looks after him sometimes if I go out and he has him some weekends. I realize now that this is all he and I had agreed, but the constant criticism of our arrangement from other people got in the way.

"I was so worried about Sam not having a traditional father at home that I forgot that many kids have really bad fathers or don't get to see their fathers at home until the weekend because they stay late at the office every night. I was beating up myself and Derek over this family image I had without looking at what I had or wanted.

"Now I've decided to make my own choices about Sam, Derek, work and anything else, and feel much more sure of myself. It's had one surprising result – my parents and I are getting on better than before. I decided to speak to them and tell them that I was pleased with having Sam. They aren't very happy with my choices, but both of them are trying not to make those comparisons with my sister all the time."

Single mothers on their own

Single mothers tend to fall into two groups: those truly on their own with their babies and those who are supported by the family club.

As a single mother on your own, all of the responsibilities – for childcare, feeding, bathing and putting to bed as well as working, shopping for food and looking after the baby at night when he or she will not stop crying – are yours and yours alone.

If you are lucky, you may arrange for or agree with someone else to help you, but all the responsibility is yours.

Having all of the responsibility for your baby and your own life may be a heavy load to carry. At the same time, it can be a distinct advantage. No one else will question your decisions or undermine your choices.

Meeting other women in the same position as you can be a great source of emotional and practical support.

Single mothers supported by their family clubs

Single mothers who are supported by members of their family club are in a fortunate but difficult position not often recognized by others. All too often, the young single mother who is helped by her own parents finds that the child's grandparents become the parents in all but name. It is easier to turn to your own mother for advice and support at first, but it has its risks. Look at "Using members of the family for childcare" in Chapter 21. By not making your own choices, you risk not developing into an adult mother.

To help you work out if there is a hidden price to pay for the help you receive, see if you answer "yes" to any of the following questions:

- Do you feel obliged to agree with your parents so they will continue to help you?
- Do you find yourself doing things for your parents instead of doing things for yourself?
- Do you often wonder whether it would be easier to pay someone else to help with childcare?
- Do you feel like a child when you are with your parents even though you are of adult age?

- Do you feel criticized or incompetent doing things for your child when your parents are watching?
- Do your parents frequently remind you how much they are doing to help you?

If you have answered "yes" to any of these questions, think about taking steps towards becoming an adult mother. Aim at developing a relationship with your parents that is one of equals. This also means recognizing that your own parents and other members of the family club have their own lives and can chose whether they help you or not.

New single mothers returning to work

Going back to work can be a mixed blessing. It returns you to the adult world, one you may not have seen much of for a while. It also forces you to have to arrange childcare on a secure basis. You do not have another adult to telephone and say, "Can you pick up Katie from childcare? I'm stuck at work."

You will need time for yourself. This need does not make you a bad mother – rather, a normal one. While you are still on maternity leave, it is worth seeking out groups for new mothers where you may find other women in the same circumstances as yourself. You may be able to swap babysitting with one of them, arranging evenings or a few hours at weekends when you will look after her baby so she can go out, and in return she will do the same for you. You should also find out about babysitting circles, paid babysitting services or anything else you can think of which may help you have a few hours off to go out and have some fun.

You are a new mother with a new baby. You may have offers of help and support from your family and friends, but be aware that these offers may disguise a need to take over decisions that should be yours concerning your child. You may have to pay a price for this at a later date. Offers of help are best formalized in some way to prevent difficulties later. You don't want the person helping with childcare to feel taken advantage of, nor do you want to feel unable to say that you are uncomfortable with something concerning your child's well-being.

Single mothers resulting from separation or divorce

Although much has been written here about new mothers returning to work following the birth of a baby, many women are faced with returning to work following separation or divorce. Their children may be much older and the women themselves may not have worked before the separation. Whatever the past arrangements, when you suddenly find yourself alone with sole responsibility for your children, everything changes.

One of the most common difficulties facing newly separated women is the feeling that they will be criticized for whatever they do. How many of these do you recognize?

- If you are not at home being the perfect mother, your ex-partner will complain that you are not raising the children properly.
- If you are not reliable at work because of emergencies at home with the children, you will be criticized and may lose your employment (and the essential salary it provides).
- If you upset the children by telling them off, you will hear the dreaded words: "I don't want to live with you any more. I want to live with . . ."
- If you upset your ex, the child maintenance payments will

be mysteriously delayed or not appear at all, causing you financial chaos.

If you try to be the perfect mother, perfect employee, perfect everything, you are doomed to failure. This is where the idea of adult motherhood is so important. You are an adult and you do have responsibilities. But at the same time, you do not have to answer to anyone else. Your ex will criticize you because he wants to hurt you. Be as firm with him as you would be with anyone else who is rude to you, and tell him what is acceptable to you now as an independent woman. Your children, too, need to know that you are sure of yourself. Their misbehaviour should be dealt with in the same way that you have always dealt with it. You are the adult mother, the head of the household, so it is important to ask yourself: "Is this acceptable to me?" If the answer is "no", act to put a stop to it.

Being alone as a parent, particularly if you have been used to sharing, can be scary and difficult. Try not to be too hard on yourself for finding it difficult – everyone does. Instead, focus on what you want for yourself and for your family.

PART FOUR

The consequences of change for visible adult mothers

23

Visible adult mothers, successful children

Being adult mothers means that we recognize our children for who and what they are – with strengths and weaknesses just like everyone else. Our children are not carbon copies of us, their parents. Neither will they be the ideal child or, later, the ideal adult we want them to be. As adult mothers, we need to step back and ask – what is good for him or her? What does she want? What makes him feel good about himself? What does she need?

Your son may take an interest in sports when you spent your own school days running away from the ball. Your daughter may choose embroidery as a means of expression and enjoyment when you always saw sewing as an example of female work that would never be a burden to *your* daughter. Children choose their own interests and hobbies. As adult parents, we can support them by taking an interest and encourage them in whatever makes them feel good and more confident in themselves. At the same time, we have to accept it when the children say, "Enough – I don't want to do this any more!" because they are still exploring, still experimenting with life.

What is a successful child?

A successful child feels good about themselves and has the

confidence to do things for him/herself. A successful child knows that actions lead to consequences, whether good or bad, and that he or she is in control of these actions. A successful child turns into a successful teenager and then a successful adult. This success is not measured in exam passes or gold medals at a particular sport. This success is measured in the life skills acquired at home, which prepare us for an independent life outside.

Perfect mothers, unsuccessful children

Perfect mothers do not raise successful children. Take the story of Daniel.

Every day Daniel runs out of school to meet his mother Jeanette at the gate. Every day she greets him with a hug and then looks down at his shoes. Every day Daniel's shoe laces are undone, so before they walk away, Jeanette bends down and ties them. As she does so, they talk about the day's events and neither thinks much of what Jeanette is doing.

At first sight, Jeanette is doing what all mothers have done. But Jeanette has been doing this every day for months! An onlooker might see her as a caring perfect mother. However, Daniel is being prevented from learning something essential to his well-being. He is denied the sense of self-care and achievement that tying his own shoe laces would bring.

Daniel runs around the playground each lunch time with his shoe laces dangling. Other children know that he cannot yet tie his own shoe laces, and as children do, they tease him. He is made to feel like a baby. Because there are other things that Daniel has not yet been given the chance to master at home, he often feels like the baby of the class. When he is given any new task to do by his teacher, he feels very anxious. What happens if he cannot do it? He does not expect to be able to do it.

How would an adult mother see Daniel? She would see him as a person who needs to learn skills to survive. She would take the time and make the effort to encourage him to learn how to tie his own shoe laces. It may take an hour a day for a school week to teach him, but for those five hours of teaching and encouragement, Jeanette would save five minutes every day for years.

Visible adult mothers allow and encourage the development of:

- Self-reliance
- Responsibility
- Emotional safety
- A sense of achievement
- A sense of belonging to a family

Self-reliance

Adult mothers are visible and self-reliant. They take time for the things they enjoy and are not afraid of new things. This acceptance of challenges, whether or not they turn out to be successes or failures, encourages the belief in the child that failing is not a disaster. The child of the adult mother will feel able to try out new things and explore new choices without feeling that not managing it this time is a failure not to be repeated.

Take Daniel. His mother Jeanette was encouraging him to remain her dependent baby without being aware of the impact this had on him. In running to take care of his every need and want, Daniel kept her constantly busy and gave her the feeling she was being a perfect mother to him. Although the tasks may change, it is likely that this pattern will continue until Daniel is a young adult. By this time, he will expect his mother always to be there to pick up after him. When he returns from a night out with his friends, she will cook for them all.

Children who have been raised by adult mothers will take pride in being able to do things for themselves. Brothers James and Douglas are 16 and 15. If their mother was trying her hardest always to be a perfect mother, she would cook all their meals and do all their laundry. All their needs would be met in the name of motherly love. But does this really meet all their needs? Within a year or two, these boys will leave home, perhaps go away to college. How will they fare when faced with washing their clothes for the first time?

Luckily for James and Douglas, theirs is an adult mother who has encouraged the boys to co-operate within the family to help with the cooking and laundry. These lessons have prepared them to go out into the adult world and do more than survive. They have been given a sense of confidence that they can cope in the world and look after themselves. When Douglas and James leave home, they will know how to keep their underpants white instead of pinky-grey and to cook themselves simple nutritious meals rather than just toast!

Responsibility

As an adult mother, you have learned to assign responsibility. Whose problem is it? When a problem is the child's responsibility, the adult mother leaves the consequences for the child to deal with.

The night before his geography project is due at secondary school, Jack tells his mother Sandra that he has not finished it. Sandra is dreadfully anxious as she wants Jack to do well at school, so she reassures Jack that all will be okay and sits down with him for an hour to work on his project. Two hours later, they are finished except for some diagrams. It is now 11pm, Jack has school in the morning and is becoming tired and irritable. Sandra sends him to bed, telling him that she will do the outstanding diagrams for him. This takes her another two hours, but as Sandra finally goes to bed at 1am, she feels that she has helped her son out of trouble and supported him in his school work.

Helping Jack has meant that Sandra missed her aerobics class. When she goes to bed, her husband is annoyed because he hasn't seen her that evening – after Sandra's aerobics class, they usually sit quietly together and talk about the day. Sandra just mentally shrugs her shoulders and wonders if Jack will be less irritable and nicer to her tomorrow. She knows that her husband will forget his annoyance by the time he wakes up!

Sandra has fulfilled her duties as a perfect mother. But whose responsibility was it to complete the geography project? Jack had been given the work two weeks before and had not made sure that it was ready to hand in when due. He may have good or bad reasons for not completing the project, but it was his responsibility to complete it.

What would an adult mother have done? She would have left the problem to Jack. The responsibility for completing the project belonged to him. The problem belonged to him. As a teenager, he needs to learn about deadlines and completing work. If he doesn't complete his project on time, his geography teacher will impose consequences, which Jack will have to deal with. Or perhaps Jack knows more than Sandra about his geography teacher. The teacher may regularly set work and then give the pupils extra time to complete it. This would mean that there would be no negative consequences to not completing the project and Jack would still be responsible for getting it in for the (second) deadline. He spends his days at school and knows how it works. He is responsible for the work he does both at school and as homework.

What can Sandra do to support Jack? As an adult mother, she can allow her son to learn the consequences of not meeting a deadline. Jack is still a teenager and has time to learn this lesson within the safety of school. An adult mother knows that learning at this stage is much safer and has fewer serious consequences than learning, say, at a first job. Getting the sack is far more serious than getting detention!

When Jack announces that he has homework to do for the next day, Sandra can support him by creating a calm atmosphere at home. Last-minute tension and panic is not productive for anyone. It does not help Jack if Sandra checks on whether he is keeping up with his homework. Once again, this is Jack's responsibility and a skill he has to learn before he leaves school.

Use the questions below to help you work out who is responsible and who should be responsible for issues to do with your children:

- Who has the problem?
- Who has the deadline?
- Who needs to do something?
- If she/he had done what she/he was supposed to, would you be involved now?
- Who gets the reward for your efforts?
- If you do not gain the reward, why are you doing it? (This may be a clue that the problem really belongs to the person you are helping or protecting.)

Emotional safety

Because adult mothers do not feel that they have to "fix" everything, their children are able to voice their feelings without fear. The child of an adult mother can say "I'm unhappy" without the mother finding this threatening or critical. This does not mean that the adult mother is unaffected. Of course, she worries. Of course, she empathizes with her child because we all want our children to be happy all of the time. But the adult mother sees her child as an individual separate from her, with up and down moods of his or her own. Sometimes simply being able to listen and empathize is enough.

All human emotions become safe for the child of an adult mother. Anger, joy, frustration and happiness are all allowed because the ownership of these feelings is the child's. Although we may be uncomfortable with the negative emotions, they are simply what the child feels at that moment.

The emotions of the perfect mother are often influenced or controlled by those around her. So if her child is angry, she feels guilt, anxiety, resentment or anger in response. The adult mother may feel all of these but recognizes what or whom is responsible for the child's feelings.

What effect does this emotional safety have on these children? They grow up learning that it is safe and acceptable to feel things and to share them with others. The natural limits to expressing ourselves, such as not smashing up furniture or reducing someone else to frightened tears, are lessons to be learned and will be taught by adult parents who are clear on how they expect to be treated. This ability to express emotion, both joy and fear, will enable children to enter into healthy relationships with friends and, later, loving partners.

A sense of achievement

The sense of achievement that children feel can only be complete if they are allowed to risk failure. So many parents, especially perfect mothers, attempt to help their children at every stage, facing any and every risk for them so that the children always succeed. However, this diminishes the children's sense of achievement because they did not do well on their own, and succeeding becomes the only reason for attempting something.

Real life is not like this. Real life is about attempting some things and failing. It is about trying some things alone, failing and still not believing that this is the end of the world or the reason never to try again. Real life is also about succeeding – alone – and so taking all the credit. An adult mother's role is to encourage, support and enable but not to take over the task or do more of it than the child.

Several years ago, my own daughter entered a library competition to design an Easter card. She designed, coloured and completed the card by herself and took much pleasure in it. On her next visit to our local library, she handed it in to the librarian. For her age group, the card was quite complicated, with a pop-up raised design on the front cover. This was something my daughter had practised and practised on pieces of card, having read how to do it in one of the books she had borrowed from the library.

I would love to tell you that she won a prize but she did not. I would love to tell you that she was not disappointed, but of course, she was. This disappointment was made worse for her when she found out that the prize winners had received lots of help from their parents. It was made even worse for me when I was told that the judges had assumed that my daughter had had lots of help with her card because of its complexity.

As a perfect mother, I might have consoled my daughter, told her how unfair it all was and even argued her case with the judges. As an adult mother, I did no such thing but rather told her what I had been told – that the card was too good for a seven-year-old to have made alone. Her reaction was interesting. Her pride and sense of achievement grew from the knowledge that others had thought her card "too good" to have been created alone. She was thrilled. The icing on the Easter cake came from the librarian, who knew of Sarah's natural talents. She had something special waiting for her the next time she visited the library – a chocolate bar. That chocolate bar meant more than the certificate for first prize.

The adult mother's sense of pride in her children, whether very young or grown, is natural. But adult mothers do not need to have their own self-pride bolstered by the achievements of their children. The children's achievements are their own, and so it is the children who gain the sense of achievement. Of course, this does not mean that a mother should never help her child with a project or task. Rather, it means that adult mothers encourage their children to do as much as possible for themselves, bolstering their independence and attempts at doing new things.

A sense of belonging to a family

The advantage of being the child of an adult mother is the strong sense of family and belonging that this can bring. At first, this may seem to be the route towards becoming a slave to the family club. However, when a child is raised within a family where people co-operate in the running of the household, support each other and do not make derogatory comments about each other, this is the family they will want to belong to. In a family with an adult mother, each person is safe to have their own achievements and failures, make their own choices and still belong. Within such supportive families, children grow up learning that they will not be rejected because of something separate from who they are, such as getting bad grades in exams or becoming pregnant while still at school. Instead these difficult events are dealt with fairly and compassionately, with the responsibility for decisions and consequences where it belongs.

24

Whatever happened to . . . ?

I always hate books that give you a snippet of someone's story and then leave you wondering what happened next. So for those of you who like to have everything nicely wrapped up, here are the answers to "whatever happened to . . . ?"

Julie

Now they were parents, Julie and Richard both took time to re-examine their relationship. Julie found that, for the time being, she was happy at home looking after Jessica, but knew that she did not want to be a full-time mum permanently. Julie and Richard worked out together how Julie could begin to attend evening classes to increase her qualifications while Jessica was still small.

There was some opposition to these plans from Julie's parents, but this time, Julie and Richard were both prepared. Julie's parents asked her if she felt tired after her classes, whether Jessica missed her and so on. When Julie was clear and firm about what she wanted and why, the questions were addressed to Richard instead. He supported Julie's decisions and made this clear to his parents-in-law. Julie and Richard were now behaving like an adult couple and adult parents. They turned to each other with their concerns and shared in decisions, and this brought them closer together.

After a few years, they decided to have another child. Julie now felt that Richard loved her and that the new child would be a welcome addition to their happy family. She continued her part-time study, and as soon as both children were at school, she started to work part-time.

For Julie, this was the perfect compromise between her own beliefs and the expectations of the family clubs that both she and Richard had grown up with – that perfect mothers stayed at home with their children.

Beverley

Beverley continued to refuse to go to school. Over the years, the family sought help from various agencies and therapists but came to accept that she suffered from a "severe school phobia". She was educated at home by a tutor and did well in her exams before officially leaving school. She continued to be helpful to her mother and do chores around the house.

There was a time when Beverley thought about going out to work at a local business and perhaps going to college, but these ideas soon proved too difficult. She found that she was unable to cope easily outside the house and later started to have panic attacks when riding the bus into town.

The answer seemed to be to stay at home. Beverley took on the role of secretary and book-keeper to the family business, which meant that she could continue to be useful to the family and did not have to leave the house. Her mother spent more time looking after Luke, who interestingly also developed the beginnings of school phobia.

Years later, all the members of this family club were still living and working under the same roof.

Anne

For a short while, Anne thought that things were going well between her and Thomas. She felt so much better now that she believed herself to be in control of her own life. She felt closer to her husband and less criticized for her way of caring for the children. But this golden time did not last.

Thomas's mother Brenda became unwell with vague aches and pains, and started to talk about how she would not be around much longer. Thomas felt terrible and blamed himself for his mother's "illness". His father told him that the strain of being so badly treated by Anne was killing his mother. Unfortunately Thomas was unable to see how unfair or untrue this was or how Brenda was re-exerting her control over him.

The conflict between Thomas and Anne increased over the following weeks as he pressured her to return to the way things had been. She had some hard choices to make. She saw that Thomas was always going to be at his mother's beck and call, even if he moaned about it at home. She also realized that this meant she would be expected always to put Brenda's needs first. Anne could see that, given a choice between herself and his mother, Thomas would choose Brenda. He would even, if Brenda cried over the telephone, choose to spend time with her rather than with his children. To Anne, this was unacceptable, and so eventually, after several separations and reconciliations, she filed for divorce. At least one of those reconciliations might have worked if Brenda had not repeatedly told Thomas how bad Anne was for him.

Interestingly, after the divorce, Thomas rapidly started a relationship with someone Brenda had always thought he should have married years before!

Dorothy

Dorothy continued to say more clearly to her husband and family how she felt and what she wanted, which, of course, took time and practice. Henry found it easier to understand Dorothy now that she was talking with him about her needs and listening in turn to his own. This is the benefit of taking responsibility for oneself.

At first Dorothy thought she was being selfish when she said, "I want . . .", but she quickly learned that this prevented anger and resentment interfering with her relationships. It continued to help her relationship with her parents, too. Her brothers and sisters were not too pleased with her change in availability, but Henry supported her and made this clear to everyone. Over the coming months and years, Dorothy and Henry continued to support her parents but also kept a separate life for themselves.

Because Dorothy did not feel drained and exhausted, she was able to enjoy visits with her friends and from her daughters far more than she had in the past. Henry continued to work for some years but finally retired. Because he and Dorothy had worked hard on improving their relationship after the girls had left home, they were able to settle into a relaxing and comfortable retirement together. And Dorothy wrote her poetry.

Lynne

Lynne told Paul that they needed to have a serious talk. She told him that she felt that, since the birth of their daughter Alice, things had not worked out the way they had talked about. Paul was shocked at how hard Lynne was finding everything, but at the same time, he did not see how he could change anything either. His career was important to him, and to ease back now on the hours he spent at work would be disastrous. He and Lynne were facing up to the harsh realities of parenthood. One or both of them had to make sacrifices to be good parents to Alice.

The first step they took to improve things was to talk and begin to appreciate how difficult their positions were for each of them. Paul took care to keep certain weekends and evenings free so that he could be with Lynne and Alice. Sometimes he would look after Alice so Lynne could go out. Sometimes they would get a babysitter and go out to have some fun together.

At work, Lynne found it easier once she had cleared the air with her colleagues. She is now enthusiastic about her job again, and because she supports her colleagues when they need her, they support her if she needs help or has to rush home to Alice. Lynne and Paul are also considering moving nearer her place of work.

After discussing their own priorities, they both decided that Lynne should have the main responsibility for Alice. Lynne feels more comfortable with this because it has been openly discussed, rather than just assumed. Now she also knows that, if she wants this to change, Paul will listen and they will work something out together.

Diana

Diana went on strike! Instead of becoming ill to get a rest, she started to say "no" to those jobs that she did not feel were her responsibility. At home, this started with her teenage daughters. She stopped picking up their clothes from the bedroom floors. She stopped doing the washing and ironing for everyone. Instead she told her daughters that they needed to learn how to use the washing machine before they left home. She showed them how to cook their favourite foods and then encouraged them to experiment in the kitchen. She made sure that they could wire an electrical plug correctly and find the fuse box in a house. Diana prepared her daughters for life in a way that she had not done before her own troubles.

Diana's husband watched with surprise as she became more confident and independent. It made him uncomfortable, but he trusted that things would settle down in a few months.

At work, Diana started to do only the part-time work that she was employed to do. This did not mean that she did not continue to work well or to the best of her ability. It did mean that she was able to set limits on how much extra time she was prepared to spend in the office and how much responsibility she should have for a task compared with the full-time staff, who were sometimes more senior. Her success at work and increased feeling of being well instead of on the edge of collapse added to Diana's confidence in herself.

Finally she spoke with her husband. She voiced all the past anger and resentment that she had felt towards him but made it clear that both of them had let things drift on for years. She asked him to support the changes she was making and talked with him about what life would be like once the girls had both left home. They started making plans for themselves. Like Dorothy and Henry in the earlier story, Diana and her husband started to prepare for the rest of their lives together.

Women taking responsibility for change

All but one of these women had reached a point in their lives when, for whatever reason, they were unhappy and could not carry on and so they would have to change. True, they found change frightening but less frightening than to continue for years with everything remaining the same.

It was only Beverley's family and, later, Beverley herself who chose to not make any changes within themselves or their family club. Even Anne – who found that the changes she wanted led her to an awful choice: continuing her relationship with Thomas with his mother clearly in control or being alone and a single parent – found that she felt better within herself as time passed.

All the women took responsibility for themselves and so made the choices that felt best to them at the time. They stopped attempting the impossible: being perfect mothers. Instead they behaved as adults, took responsibility as adults and thus became effective, visible adult mothers in their own right.

Further help and support

Recommended reading and viewing

Novels

Chopin, K (1996). *The Awakening*. Cambridge: Cambridge University Press.

Hardy, T (1994). *Jude the Obscure*. London: Penguin Popular Classics.

Weldon, F (1984). *The Life and Loves of a She-Devil*. London: Coronet Books.

Waller, R J (1993). *The Bridges of Madison County*. New York: Mandarin.

Examinations of the position of women

Estes, P C (1992). *Women who Run with the Wolves*. New York: Ballantine Books.

Faludi, S (1992). *Backlash*. London: Chatto & Windus.

Wolf, N (1991). *The Beauty Myth*. New York: Anchor Books.

Wolf, N (1997). *Promiscuities*. London: Chatto & Windus.

Self-help books

Dickson, A (1982). *A Woman in Your Own Right*. London: Quartet Books.

Fahey, T and Hutchinson, G (1992). *Weight Training for Women*. Mayfield Publishing.

Forward, S (1990). *Toxic Parents*. London: Bantam Books.

Forward, S (1997). *Emotional Blackmail*. London: Bantam Press.

Lerner, H G (1985). *The Dance of Anger*. London: HarperCollins.

Lerner, H G (1989). *The Dance of Intimacy*. London: HarperCollins.

Lerner, H G (1993). *The Dance of Deception*. London: HarperCollins.

Lerner, H G (1999). *The Mother Dance*. London: HarperCollins.

Litvinoff, S (1992). *The Relate Guide to Better Relationships*. London: Vermillion.

Ussher, J (1991). *Women's Madness: misogyny or mental illness?* London: HarvesterWheatsheaf.

Films

Avnet, J (director) (1991). *Fried Green Tomatoes at the Whistlestop Café*.

Recommended reading and viewing

Eastwood, C (director) (1995). *Bridges of Madison County*.

Haywood-Carter, A (director) (1996). *Foxfire*.

Ross, G (director) (1998). *Pleasantville*.

Support and self-help groups

Assertiveness groups
Enquire at your local community college.

British Association for Counselling
1 Regent Place
Rugby
Warwickshire
CV21 2PJ
Tel: 01788 550 899
Information on counsellors in your area.

British Psychological Society
48 Princess Road East
Leicester
LE1 7DR
Tel: 0116 254 9568
Information on psychologists in your area.

Citizens' Advice Bureaux
Useful information about support groups and classes in your area. You can find the contact details of the CAB nearest you in your local telephone book.

MIND: The National Association for Mental Health
15–19 Broadway
London E15 4BQ
Tel: 0345 660 163
Useful information about support groups and classes in your area.

Parentline
Tel: 01702 559 900
Helpline for parents and other carers of children.

Refuge
Tel: 020 8995 4430
24-hour crisis line providing practical advice and emotional support for women experiencing domestic violence.

Samaritans
Tel: 0345 909090
Someone to talk to any time of the day or night. They are not there just for those thinking of suicide but as an impartial listening ear for all of us when we need one.

Your thoughts and comments about this book

- If you have an interesting story to tell . . .
- If you found this book useful . . .
- If you have any comments to make . . .
- If you can think of a topic that should have been in this book . . .

write to:

Susan Van Scoyoc, c/o Constable & Robinson Ltd,
3 The Lanchesters, 162 Fulham Palace Road, London W6 9ER
Email: enquiries@constablerobinson.com

Notes

1   Malhotra, I, *Indira Gandhi: A personal and political biography*. Boston: Northeastern University Press, 1989, p. 26.

2   Morton, Andrew, *Diana: Her true story*. London: Michael O'Mara Books, 1992.

3   Matlin, M W, *The Psychology of Women*. London: Harcourt Brace Jovanovich College Publishers, 2nd ed. 1993, p. 37.

4   "Dear Vicky: I can't tolerate my wife anymore", *The Yellow Advertiser* (Basildon, Essex), 8 January 1999, p. 15.

5   Matlin, M W, *op. cit.*, p. 45.

6   *Ibid.*, p. 47.

7   Pilcher, J Student, "Harassment", Associated Press, 11 January 1999.

8   Silverstein, B & Perlick, D,*The Cost of Competence: Why inequality causes depression, eating disorders and illness in women*. Oxford: Oxford University Press, 1995.

9   Thanks to Bonnie Peisner and Ann Oortman for permission to use these letters.

10 "Anxious mums-to-be may have smaller babies", *Yahoo News*, 15 January 1999.

11   Craig, O, "Why leave? Mum does the washing, Dad pays the bills", *Sunday Telegraph* (London), 28 March 1999.

12   Office for National Statistics, UK.

13   MIND: The National Association for Mental Health. Thank you to training officer Louise Flory for all her help.

14   *Ibid*.

15   *Woman's Body: An owner's manual*. London: Corgi Books, 1978, p. 139.

16   Lerner, H G, *Life Preservers*, New York: HarperCollins, 1996.

17   Winnicott, D W, *Home Is Where We Start From: Essays by a psychoanalyst*. Norton, 1990. A collection of essays by this well-respected psychoanalyst who focused on mothers and children in much of his work.

18   Fahey, T & Hutchinson, G, *Weight Training for Women*. Mayfield Publishing, 1992.

Index

Index

Index